The Five Languages
of
Apology

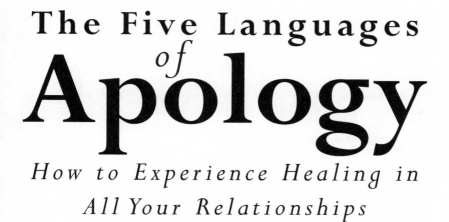

The Five Languages

of

Apology

*How to Experience Healing in
All Your Relationships*

GARY CHAPMAN
JENNIFER THOMAS

NORTHFIELD PUBLISHING
CHICAGO

Cover and Interior Design: Smartt Guys design
Cover Image: ©David Muir / Masterfile
Editors: Jim Vincent and Elizabeth Cody Newenhuyse

Library of Congress Cataloging-in-Publication Data

Chapman, Gary D., 1938-
    The five languages of apology : how to experience healing in all your relationships /
Gary Chapman and Jennifer Thomas.
        p. cm.
    Includes bibliographical references.
    ISBN-13: 978-1-881273-57-8
    1. Apologizing. I. Thomas, Jennifer, 1969- II. Title.

BF575.A75.C43 2006
158.2—dc22

                                                                2006009739

ISBN: 1-881273-57-1
ISBN-13: 978-1-881273-57-8

We hope you enjoy this book from Northfield Publishing. Our goal is to provide high-quality, thought-provoking books and products that connect truth to your real needs and challenges. For more information on other books and products written and produced from a biblical perspective, go to www.moodypublishers.com or write to:

Northfield Publishing
820 N. LaSalle Boulevard
Chicago, IL 60610

1 3 5 7 9 10 8 6 4 2

Printed in the United States of America

To Karolyn, who has accepted my apologies and extended forgiveness
many times through our four decades
as husband and wife

————————

To J.T., my husband and ally,
who has shared my dreams
and helped make them come true

Other Books by Gary Chapman

The Five Love Languages
The Five Love Languages of Children
The Five Love Languages of Teenagers
The Five Love Languages for Singles
The Love Languages of God
Your Gift of Love
Parenting Your Adult Child
The Other Side of Love
Loving Solutions
Five Signs of a Loving Family
Dr. Gary Chapman on the Marriage You've Always Wanted
A Couple's Guide to a Growing Marriage
The World's Easiest Guide to Family Relationships
Hope for the Separated
Covenant Marriage
The Four Seasons of Marriage

Contents

Acknowledgments

W e would need to apologize if we did not acknowledge our appreciation for the hundreds of couples who took time to complete our apology questionnaire and for the scores who gave us extensive interviews. Without their help, this book could not have been written. Many of these couples spoke honestly of their own failures at apologizing and forgiving. Others shared the journey that led them to discovering the art of apologizing effectively and finding the joy of reconciliation. The book is enriched by the honesty of these couples.

Both of us are also indebted to the couples and individuals who have turned to us for counsel. Many of the clients who have sat in our offices have been there because someone failed to apologize. Their stories have taught us the pain of rejection and, in some cases, the joy of seeing them learn how to give and receive an apology and thus open the door to forgiveness and reconciliation. We have changed their names and certain details to protect their privacy, but their stories add much to this book.

A special thanks to Tricia Kube, who computerized the manuscript and gave us great encouragement; to Shannon Warden, who created the "apology profile" found at the end of the book and who also was a great help in collecting and organizing our research questionnaires; and to Kay Tatum, our technical guru who made the manuscript presentable for the publisher.

We are also grateful to Greg Thornton and the wonderful team at Moody Publishers, who not only did a superb job in editing the book, but also gave us much encouragement as we did our research and writing.

Finally, we each want to thank our spouses, Karolyn and J.T., to whom we dedicate this volume. Without their love and support, neither of us would have had the emotional energy to complete the project. This book is a tribute to their generous spirits.

GARY D. CHAPMAN, Ph.D.
JENNIFER M. THOMAS, Ph.D.

Introduction

Minutes before my marriage seminar was to begin on a Saturday morning in Spokane, Jean walked up to me and introduced herself. "Dr. Chapman, my husband and I have driven up from California. We are excited about being here, but I want to ask you one question. Are you going to deal with the importance of apologizing?"

"That's an interesting topic," I responded. "Why do you ask?"

"Well, all my husband says is 'I'm sorry.' To me, that's not an apology."

"So what do you want him to say or do?" I asked.

"I want him to admit that he is wrong and to ask me to forgive him. I also want him to assure me that it won't happen again."

I smiled and said, "I'm very glad that you shared this with me, because I am currently doing research on the subject of apologizing."

"Really?" she said, her eyes revealing keen interest.

"Yes. I have the idea that what one person considers an apology is not what another person considers to be an apology. You have just illustrated the concept. Perhaps for your husband, saying 'I'm sorry' is a sincere apology, but obviously, that is not your perception of an apology."

"That's right," she said. "It's got to be more than 'I'm sorry.' I don't even know what he is sorry for."

"I would really like for you and your husband to fill out one of the research forms that I'll be giving out later today. I'm trying to determine how common it is for husbands and wives to have different perceptions of apologizing. Your comments would be very helpful to me."

I walked away from that conversation convinced that I must continue my research. I also recalled the day eighteen months earlier when Dr. Jennifer Thomas sat in my office and shared her idea that men and women speak languages of apology. "I have read your book on the five love languages. My husband and I found it extremely helpful in our own relationship," she said. She added that she uses the concept in her counseling of other couples.

"The idea that each of us has a primary love language and if that language is not spoken we do not feel loved has opened the eyes of a lot of my clients. I have watched them learn to speak each other's love language and have observed how the emotional climate in the marriage improves. It is a very practical tool to help couples learn how to connect to each other emotionally and, as you say in the book, to keep each other's love tanks full." As an author whose love language is *words of affirmation*, I was enjoying Jennifer's accolades, but I was not prepared for what she said next.

"I believe that people also have different ways of apologizing, and what one person considers a sincere apology is not what another person may consider a sincere apology. In essence, they have different languages of apology.

"I have seen this often in my counseling. One spouse says, 'If he/she would only apologize,' and the other says, 'I have apologized.' 'No, you haven't,' the other one says. 'You have never admitted that you are wrong.' So they get into an argument about what it means to apologize. Obviously, they have different perceptions."

I was immediately intrigued with the idea. I remembered numerous couples in my office exhibiting similar behavior. It was obvious they were not connecting with each other. The supposed apology was not having the desired effect of forgiveness and reconciliation. I also remembered occasions in my own marriage when Karolyn had apologized but I considered it rather weak, and other occasions when I had apologized, but she had a hard time forgiving me because she felt that I was insincere.

I said to Jennifer, "I think you are on to something. Your idea certainly resonates with my experience. What do you plan to do with this idea?"

"I'd like to write an article," she said, "and I was wondering if you could help me get it published."

"I'd be glad to," I said. "Why don't you write the article, send me a copy, and we'll go from there?"

The next week, Jennifer's idea kept coming back to me again and again. In fact, that very week I encountered a couple in my office who were disagreeing on whether the husband had genuinely apologized. The wife was having difficulty forgiving him because, in her mind, he had never apologized, while he was convinced that he had apologized. A week later, I called Jennifer's office and said to her, "I've been thinking about your idea and I think it is bigger than an article. Would you be open to the possibility of the two of us doing research on apologies and perhaps writing a book together on the subject?" She was elated and I was delighted, because I knew her idea had tremendous potential for helping couples to find forgiveness and reconciliation.

Two years later, after much research, we have now written this book, *The Five Languages of Apology*. Our research has clearly revealed that when it comes to apologizing, people indeed speak different languages. That is why sincere apologies may not always be received as sincere, and why forgiveness and reconciliation are not always forthcoming. From our observations as marital therapists, we notice a deafening lack of persuasive apologies. We believe that the shortage of apologies with impact may be a central factor in the epidemic of crumbling marriages that we see today. There are several good resources regarding apologies that are currently available. To the best of our knowledge, however, this book is the first attempt to shape the content of an apology to the particular needs (or language) of the recipient.

Jennifer and I have worked together in collecting and analyzing the research data on which this book is based. We agreed that for clarity and continuity, I (Gary) would write the book and Jennifer would prepare illustrations of the concepts taken from our research and her own experience as a professional counselor. These will be clearly identified in the text as coming from her. It is our desire that as you read the book, you will hear one voice and two hearts beating together in an effort to communicate a message that we both believe has great potential for enhancing relationships.

In the first half of this book, we will identify and describe each of the five languages of an apology. The second half of the book will illustrate how the concept can enhance relationships in marriages, in parenting, in families, in dating relationships, and at work.

Of course, apologies affect people in larger settings as well. So in chapter 3 we will address one unique televised apology (by Oprah Winfrey), and in chapter 4 we will note two national apologies (the United States to Japanese Americans and Germany to Holocaust survivors).

We will conclude with a chapter that some may see as ethereal but we believe holds great potential: What would the world be like if we all learned to apologize effectively?

The FIVE LANGUAGES
of APOLOGY

EXPRESSING REGRET
"I am sorry"

ACCEPTING RESPONSIBILITY
"I was wrong"

MAKING RESTITUTION
"What can I do to make it right?"

GENUINELY REPENTING
"I'll try not to do that again"

REQUESTING FORGIVENESS
"Will you please forgive me?"

1

Why **APOLOGIZE?**

In a perfect world, there would be no need for apologies. But because the world is imperfect, we cannot survive without them. My academic background is the field of anthropology, the study of human culture. One of the clear conclusions of the anthropologist is that all people have a sense of morality: Some things are right, and some things are wrong. People are incurably moral. In psychology, it is often called the conscience. In theology, it may be referred to as the "sense of *ought*" or the imprint of the divine.

It is true that the standard by which the conscience condemns or affirms is influenced by the culture. For example, in Eskimo (or Inuit) culture, if one is on a trek and runs out of food, it is perfectly permissible to enter the igloo of a stranger and eat whatever is available. In most other Western cultures, to enter an unoccupied house would be considered "breaking and entering," an offense punishable as a crime. Although the standard of right will differ from culture to culture and sometimes within cultures, all people have a sense of right and wrong.

When one's sense of right is violated, that person will experience anger. He or she will feel wronged and resentful at the person who has violated their trust. The wrongful act stands as a barrier between the two people, and the relationship is fractured. They cannot, even if they desired, live as though the wrong had not been committed. Something inside the offended calls for justice. It is these human realities that serve as the basis of all judicial systems.

A Cry for Reconciliation

While justice may bring some sense of satisfaction to the offended person, justice does not typically restore relationships. If an employee who is found stealing from the company is caught, tried, and fined or imprisoned, everyone says, "Justice has been served." But the company is not likely to restore the employee to the original place of leadership. On the other hand, if an employee steals from the company but quickly takes responsibility for the error, reports that misdeed to the supervisor, expresses sincere regret, offers to pay for all inequities, and pleads for mercy, there is the possibility that the employee will be allowed to continue with the company.

Humankind has an amazing capacity to forgive. I remember a number of years ago visiting the town of Coventry, England. I stood in the shell of a cathedral that had been bombed by the Nazis in the Second World War. I listened as the guide told the story of the new cathedral that rose beside the ruins. Some years after the war, a group of Germans had come and helped build the new cathedral as an act of contrition for the damages their fellow countrymen had inflicted. Everyone had agreed to allow the ruins to remain in the shadow of the new cathedral. Both structures were symbolic: the one of inhumanity between humans, the other of the power of forgiveness and reconciliation.

Something within us cries out for reconciliation when wrongdoing has fractured a relationship. The desire for reconciliation is often more potent than the desire for justice. The more intimate the relationship, the deeper the desire for reconciliation. When a husband treats his wife unfairly, in her hurt and anger she is pulled between a longing for justice and a desire for mercy. On the one hand, she wants him to pay for his wrongdoing; on the other hand, she wishes for reconciliation. It is his sincere apology that makes genuine reconciliation possible. If there is no apology, then her sense of morality pushes her to demand justice. Many times through the years I have observed divorce proceedings and watched the judge seek to determine what was just. I have often wondered if sincere apologies would have changed the sad outcome.

FOR LACK OF AN APOLOGY . . .

I have looked into the eyes of teenage rage and wondered how different life would be if an abusive father had apologized. Teenage violence toward parents can be traced to two sources. First, the teenager feels wronged by the parents and has never been reconciled. Second, the teenager feels unloved by the parents. In an earlier book, I dealt with the topic "How to love teenagers effectively."[1] In this book, we will deal with "How to apologize to teenagers effectively."

The need for apologies permeates all human relationships. Marriage, parenting, dating, and vocational relationships all require apologies. Without apologies, anger builds and pushes us to demand justice. When, as we see it, justice is not forthcoming, we often take matters into our own hands and seek revenge on those who have wronged us. Anger escalates and can end in violence. The man who walks into the office of his former employer and shoots his supervisor and three of his coworkers is typically not mentally unbalanced. That is evidenced by the fact that his neighbors are often shocked that he would do such a thing. He "seemed so normal."

He is, rather, a man who burns with a sense of injustice—to the point where only murderous revenge will right the wrong. Things

might have been different had he had the courage to lovingly confront
—and others had the courage to apologize.

In marriages, domestic turmoil is often rooted in an unwillingness to apologize. The wife says, "He treats me like dirt and then
wants to jump in bed with me. How could he do that?" while the husband responds, "She treats me like a child and wants to control my
life. I didn't marry her to get a second mother." Both are hurt; both
are angry; and both have failed, but neither is willing to apologize.
For lack of an apology, they declare war, which sometimes lasts for
years and often ends in divorce or death. Partners in healthy marriages are willing to apologize.

CAN YOU FORGIVE WITHOUT AN APOLOGY?

Genuine forgiveness and reconciliation are two-person transactions
that are enabled by apologies. Some, particularly within the Christian
worldview, have taught forgiveness without an apology. They often
quote the words of Jesus, "If you do not forgive men their trespasses,
neither will your Father forgive your trespasses."[2] Thus, they say to
the wife whose husband has been unfaithful and continues in his adul-
terous affair, "You must forgive him, or God will not forgive you."
Such an interpretation of Jesus' teachings fails to reckon with the rest
of the scriptural teachings on forgiveness. The Christian is instructed
to forgive others in the same manner that God forgives us. How does
God forgive us? The Scriptures say that if we confess our sins, God
will forgive our sins.[3] Nothing in the Old or New Testaments indicates that God forgives the sins of people who do not confess and
repent of their sins.

When a pastor encourages a wife to forgive her erring husband
while he still continues in his wrongdoing, the minister is requiring
of the wife something that God Himself does not do. Jesus' teaching
is that we are to be always willing to forgive, as God is always willing
to forgive, those who repent. Some will object to this idea, indicating

that Jesus forgave those who were killing Him. But that is not what the Scriptures say. Rather, Jesus prayed, "Father, forgive them, for they do not know what they are doing."[4] Jesus expressed His heart of compassion and His desire to see His murderers forgiven. That should be our desire and our prayer. But their forgiveness came later when they acknowledged that they had indeed killed the Son of God.[5]

Forgiveness without an apology is often encouraged for the benefit of the forgiver rather than the benefit of the offender. Such forgiveness does not lead to reconciliation. When there is no apology, the Christian is encouraged to release the person to God for justice[6] and to release one's anger to God through forbearance.[7] Dietrich Bonhoeffer, the great theologian who was martyred by the Nazis in a concentration camp in 1945, argued against the "preaching of forgiveness without requiring repentance." He referred to such forgiveness as "cheap grace . . . which amounts to the justification of sin without the justification of the repentant sinner."[8]

Genuine forgiveness removes the barrier that was created by the offense and opens the door to restoring trust over time. If the relationship was warm and intimate before the offense, it can become loving again. If the relationship was simply one of casual acquaintance, it may grow to a deeper level through the dynamic process of forgiveness. If the offense was created by an unknown person such as a rapist or a murderer, there was no relationship to be restored. If they have apologized and you have forgiven, each of you is free to go on living your lives, although the criminal will still face the judicial system created by the culture to deal with deviant behavior.

THE FIVE-GALLON CONTAINER

When we apologize, we accept responsibility for our behavior, seeking to make amends with the person who was offended. Genuine apology opens the door to the possibility of forgiveness and reconciliation. Then we can continue to build the relationship. Without apology, the offense sits as a barrier, and the quality of the relationship is diminished. Good relationships are always marked by a willingness to apologize, forgive, and reconcile. The reason many relationships are cold and distant is because we have failed to apologize.

Sincere apologies also assuage a guilty conscience. Picture your conscience as a five-gallon container strapped to your back. Whenever you wrong another, it's like pouring a gallon of liquid into your conscience. Three or four wrongs and your conscience is getting full —and you are getting heavy. A full conscience leaves one with a sense of guilt and shame. The only way to effectively empty the conscience is to apologize to God and the person you offended. When this is done, you can look God in the face, you can look yourself in the mirror, and you can look the other person in their eyes; not because you are perfect but because you have been willing to take responsibility for your failure.

We may or may not have learned the art of apologizing when we were children. In healthy families, parents teach their children to apologize. However, many children grow up in dysfunctional families where hurt, anger, and bitterness are a way of life and no one ever apologizes.

CAN WE LEARN TO APOLOGIZE?

The good news is that the art of apology can be learned. What we have discovered in our research is that there are five fundamental aspects of an apology. We call them the five languages of apology. Each of them is important. But for a particular individual, one or two of the languages may communicate more effectively than the others. The key to good relationships is learning the apology language of the other person and being willing to speak it. When you speak their primary language, you make it easier for them to genuinely forgive you. When you fail to speak their language, it makes forgiveness more difficult because they are not sure if you are genuinely apologizing.

Understanding and applying the five languages of an apology will greatly enhance all of your relationships.

In the next five chapters, we will explain the five languages. And in chapter 7, we will show you how to discover both your own and another person's primary apology language and how this can make your efforts at apologizing most productive. The balance of the book will look at the challenges in apologizing, forgiving, and then using the languages of apology in all of your relationships.

Love Story, a popular movie of the 1970s, included the famous line, "Love means never having to say you're sorry." No; it's just the opposite. Love often means saying you're sorry, and real love will include apologies by the offender and forgiveness by the offended. This is the path to restored, loving relationships. It all begins by learning to speak the right language of apology when you offend someone.

The FIVE LANGUAGES *of* APOLOGY

EXPRESSING REGRET
"I am sorry"

ACCEPTING RESPONSIBILITY
"I was wrong"

MAKING RESTITUTION
"What can I do to make it right?"

GENUINELY REPENTING
"I'll try not to do that again"

REQUESTING FORGIVENESS
"Will you please forgive me?"

A P O L O G Y   L A N G U A G E   # 1

Expressing **REGRET**

O n the evening of April 6, 2005, I was watching two television programs concurrently. On one channel Larry King
was interviewing Jane Fonda on her book *My Life So Far*
(Random House). On the other network Alan Colmes was interviewing Oliver North, who was talking about the "acts of treason" that he
alleged Jane Fonda had perpetrated during the Vietnam War.

Alan said, "But she apologized," to which Oliver North replied,
"No, she did not apologize."

"She said that she was sorry," Alan responded.

"That's not an apology," said North, adding, "She didn't say 'Will
you forgive me?' 'I'm sorry' is not an apology."

In addition to their political differences, Oliver North and Alan
Colmes clearly do not agree on what constitutes an apology. The message of this book is that people often speak different languages of
apology.

What most people are looking for in an apology is sincerity. They want the apology to be genuine, but how do you determine sincerity? Therein lies the problem. The evidence of sincerity differs from person to person. What one person considers to be sincere is not what another person considers to be sincere.

Our research has led us to the conclusion that there are five basic elements of an apology. We call them the five languages of an apology. For most people, one or two of these speak more deeply of sincerity than the others. You do not need to include all five languages to offer an effective apology. For an apology to be accepted, you need to speak the language (or perhaps two languages) that conveys to the offended your sincerity. Then he or she will regard your apology as genuine and will likely accept it.

The first language of apology is *expressing regret*. Most commonly, it is expressed in the words "I am sorry." Expressing regret is the emotional aspect of an apology. It is expressing to the offended person your own sense of guilt, shame, and pain that your behavior has hurt him deeply. It is interesting that when Robert Fulghum wrote his book *All I Really Need to Know I Learned in Kindergarten*, he included as one of the things he learned: "Say you're sorry when you hurt somebody."[1] Expressing regret is fundamental to good relationships.

Apology is birthed in the womb of regret. We regret the pain we have caused, the disappointment, the inconvenience, the betrayal of trust. Regret focuses on what you did or failed to do and how it affected the other person. The offended one is experiencing painful emotions, and they want you to feel some of their pain. They want some evidence that you realize how deeply you have hurt them. For some people, this is the one thing they listen for in an apology. Without the expression of regret, they do not sense that the apology is adequate or sincere.

SAYING THE MAGIC WORDS

A simple "I'm sorry" can go a long way toward restoring goodwill. The absence of the words "I'm sorry" stands out to some like a very sore thumb. Quite often offenders will not realize that they have left out some "magic words," but you can be assured that the listener is scanning the silence for those missing words.

Let me (Jennifer) share a personal story. Last spring I was part of a group of women who received end-of-the-year prizes for each having led a small group. I selected my prize from a sales consultant's catalog and was eagerly awaiting the arrival of my thank-you gift. The summer came and went with no delivery of my product. I began to wonder, *Where is my order?* When the end of the year came with no package, I concluded that my order was not likely to come. I actually decided at that time that it was not worth pursuing the issue with anyone. I reasoned that I had enjoyed leading the group and put the item out of my mind with the refrain, "Easy come, easy go."

Imagine my surprise when I received a telephone message from the consultant the next spring. She said that she had been cleaning out boxes and found my order! She closed the phone message by saying simply that she wanted to arrange to get the item to me. For my part, I was pleasantly surprised to be in the position to receive that which I had let go. However, something was nagging at me. I replayed her message and confirmed my suspicion: She had failed to say, "I am sorry for my mistake," or to express any sort of regret. I would have quickly embraced such an apology.

As it was, I pondered the issue in my mind long enough to write it down and to wonder how often I might do the same thing. Do I correct problems, yet not assume responsibility or express regret? The magic words "I am sorry" would have made a world of difference to me.

Many people can identify with Jennifer's experience. Karen lives in Duluth, Minnesota. She has been married to her husband, Jim, for twenty-seven years. When I (Gary) asked her, "What do you look for in an apology when Jim has wronged you?" her immediate response was, "Most of all I want him to understand how he hurt me and why. I want him to see things from my perspective. I expect to hear him say, 'I apologize. I am really sorry.'

"It helps if he gives an explanation of how his actions have hurt me. That way, I know he understands. If it is something really bad, I expect abject misery and want him to really be sad about the pain he caused me."

I asked, "When you say 'really bad,' what kind of things do you have in mind?"

"Like the time he took a girl at the office out to lunch without telling me. I heard it from a friend, and I was really hurt. I think if he had tried to justify it, I would have never gotten over it. You see, my husband is not the kind of man who takes other women out to lunch. I knew he had to have a little fascination for her or he would not have done it. He admitted that I was right and told me how sorry he was. He said that he knew that I would never go out with another man and that if I did, he would be deeply hurt. He said that he regretted what he had done and wished he had never done it. I knew he was sincere when I saw tears come to his eyes." For Karen, the heart of an apology is a sincere expression of regret.

WHAT DOES YOUR BODY SAY?

It is important that our body language agree with the words we are saying if we expect the offended person to sense our sincerity. Karen mentioned Jim's tears as evidence of his sincerity. Listen to the words of another wife who said, "I know when my husband sincerely feels sorry for something he's done, because he becomes very quiet and his physical mannerisms become introverted. He apologizes with a soft voice and a bowed head. This shows me that he feels really bad. Then I know it's genuine."

Robert and Katie have been married for seven years. When I asked him, "How do you know that Katie is sincere when she apologizes?" his answer was, "Eye contact. If she looks me in the eye and says 'I'm sorry,' I know she's sincere. If she says 'I'm sorry' while passing through the room, I know she's hiding something. A hug and a kiss after the apology also let me know that she's sincere."

Robert is illustrating the reality that sometimes our body language speaks louder than our spoken language. This is especially true when the two contradict each other. For example, one wife said, "When he screams at me, 'I said I'm sorry,' but his eyes are glaring and his hands are shaking, it's like he's trying to make me forgive him. It seems to me he is more concerned about moving on and forgetting it than truly apologizing. It's like my hurt doesn't matter—let's just get on with life."

SORRY FOR WHAT?

An apology has more impact when it's specific. LuAnn captured this idea when she said, "I expect the apologizer to say 'I'm sorry for_____' and then be specific about what they are sorry about." When we're specific, we communicate to the offended person that we truly understand how much we have hurt him or her. Specificity places the focus on our action and how it affected the other person.

And the more details we can give, the better. If I (Jennifer) stood someone up for a movie, I wouldn't just say, "I'm sorry I didn't make it to the movie." It would mean more to the person if I could list all the ways my action affected her. "I know that you left your home on time; you stopped what you were doing. You made it down here during rush-hour traffic; you had to wait and be concerned about my well-being. I know that you like to see the entire picture, and for you, my neglect may have made you unable to enjoy the movie since you missed the beginning. I can imagine how upset I would have been if a friend had done this to me. You have a right to be angry, disappointed, frustrated, and hurt—and I want you to know that I am sincerely sorry for my irresponsibility."

The details reveal the depth of your understanding of the situation and how much you inconvenienced your friend.

AVOIDING THE 'BUT . . .'

Sincere regret also needs to stand alone. It should not be followed with "But . . ." Rodney, who has been married three years to his second wife, says, "I know that my wife's apology is sincere when she says, 'I'm sorry. I know that I hurt you by yelling at you.' Then she does not go on to accuse me of causing her to get upset. My first wife always blamed me for everything."

Numerous individuals in our research made statements similar to this. "She apologizes, then blames her actions on something I did to provoke her. Blaming me does little to make the apology sincere."

Brenda remembers well one of her husband's failed attempts at apologizing—it happened the night before they would attend one of my marriage seminars. Her husband went to a coworker's fiftieth birthday party, leaving Brenda at home with their four children. Because her husband normally worked a 10 p.m. to 6 a.m. shift, she had hoped for valuable evening time together.

"Even though I was angry, he left and said that he would be back in an hour," Brenda recalls. "Two and one-half hours later when we were all in bed, he shows up. He apologized but added that I was acting like a baby and he has a right to go out.

"So whatever words he was saying to apologize weren't helping, since he was putting me down. I also prayed that when he got home, I wouldn't have a bad attitude. But I was so filled with anger that it didn't work."

Anytime we verbally shift the blame to the other person, we have moved from an apology to an attack. Attacks never lead to forgiveness and reconciliation.

Joanne is a twenty-seven-year-old single who has been in a committed dating relationship for three years. She said, "Anytime an apology is followed by an excuse for the offense, the excuse cancels out the apology in my mind. Just own up that, intentionally or not, you hurt me or didn't meet my expectations. Don't apologize and then make excuses for your offense. Leave it at the apology."

As sisters, Iris and Marie were often in conflict. They each wanted to have a better relationship, but neither seemed to know how. When I asked Marie, "Does Iris ever apologize when she loses her temper?" Marie said yes. "She apologizes all the time, but she usually ends her apology with 'I just wish you would stop putting me down. I know I am not as educated as you, but that doesn't mean that you can treat me like dirt.' What kind of an apology is that? She puts all the blame on me.

"I think she must have real struggles with self-esteem. At any rate, her apologies come across as attacks on me."

APOLOGIES THAT DO NOT MANIPULATE

An expression of sincere regret should not manipulate the other person into reciprocating. Doug and Nancy have been dating for two years and are going through some rough waters. She said, "Doug has at times said he was sorry. But then he expects me to say it back, even if I don't feel like I should have to because *he* was the cause of the fight in the first place. That just doesn't work for me. I want him to say he's sorry and not expect anything in return. That would mean that he is truly sorry."

Sometimes we hurt people and don't realize it. It was certainly not intentional. Good relationships are fostered by expressing regret even when we did not intend to hurt them. If I bump into someone getting out of an elevator, I say "I'm sorry," not because I intentionally bumped him, but because I identify with his inconvenience or irritation with my unintentional bump. The same principle is true in close relationships. You may not realize that your behavior has upset your spouse, but when it becomes apparent, then you can say, "I'm sorry that my behavior caused you so much pain. I didn't intend to hurt you."

Regret focuses on dealing with one's own behavior and expressing empathy for the hurt it has caused the other person. Insincerity is also communicated when we say "I'm sorry" simply to get the other person to stop confronting us with the issue. Rhonda sensed this when she said, "Early in our marriage, my husband did something really damaging. He absolutely refused to be sorry or repent. Then eventually he said that he was sorry, but it was only to get me off his back. His actions spoke more loudly than his words, indicating: 'Drop it! I want to get out of this trap.' He didn't see that what he had done was wrong and hurt me deeply."

'I HOPE YOU CAN FORGIVE ME'

Writing a letter of apology may help to underscore your sincerity. To put your apology in writing may give it more emotional weight, because your spouse or friend can read it again and again. The process of writing may also help you clarify your regrets and verbalize them in a positive way. Here is a letter that one of my (Jennifer's) clients received from her husband. She has given me permission to share it.

Dear Olivia,

I want to apologize for being late tonight and for not letting you know as soon as I could anticipate that I would be late again. I know this was an awfully difficult day for you with the kids. I wish so much I could have been here to help, or at least been on time to relieve you. My heart broke when at 6:30 p.m. I got your message from 4:45 p.m. with your cry for help and request that I be home on time. I hated to think that every moment from then on you must have been listening for my return. I really regret that my not setting good boundaries with my boss forced you to carry an extra burden today. I will strive to be more reliable. I am sorry, and I hope you can forgive me.

With contrition, your loving husband,

Jim

Olivia wrote at the bottom of the page, "Forgiven on 1/20/05." Obviously, Jim's expression of regret got through to Olivia. She sensed his sincerity and was willing to forgive him.

For some individuals, receiving a sincere expression of regret is the strongest language of apology. It is what convinces them that the apology is sincere. Without it, they will hear your words but they will appear empty. Their primary apology language is sincere words of regret. When they hear them, they are fully willing to forgive. Without them, forgiveness becomes difficult.

THE POWER OF APOLOGY LANGUAGE #1

Look at what the following individuals had to say about apology language #1: *expressing regret.*

"My husband had made comments in front of our friends about my being overweight and eating too much. I was deeply hurt. Later that night, he said that he knew the situation was very uncomfortable for me and he was sorry for what he had done to create the situation by his hurtful words. I forgave him because I felt he was sincere."

—Marilyn, age fifty-three, married eleven years
to her second husband

"I want an apology that comes from the heart, that is truly sorry for the action that caused my hurt. In other words, I want them to feel bad for making me feel bad."

—Vicky, age twenty-six and single

"He came home late one night, but he apologized for disappointing me. I told him it was OK; I understood. He continued by saying that he still did not like to disappoint me; that made me feel really good."

—Catina, age twenty-eight, married two years

"[It's a genuine apology] when she expresses true feelings of regret, expresses understanding of my feelings and acts like she is sorry that she hurt me."

—Ted, age forty, married for twenty years

When asked, "What do you look for in an apology?" Bob responded, "True remorse. I want to see that they feel guilty for what they did or said and are truly sorry."

—Bob, age thirty-four and single

For these and many others, the apology language of expressing regret is extremely important in the process of healing and restoration. If you want these people to sense your sincerity, then you must learn to speak the language of regret, which focuses on their pain and your behavior and how the two are related. It is communicating to them that you feel hurt because you know your actions have hurt them. It is this identification with their pain that stimulates in them a willingness to forgive.

If you are willing to express regret, here are some statements that may help you do so.

STATEMENTS OF REGRET

♥ *I know now that I hurt you very deeply. That causes me immense pain. I am truly sorry for what I did.*

♥ *I feel really bad that I disappointed you. I should have been more thoughtful. I'm sorry that I caused you so much pain.*

♥ *At the time, obviously I was not thinking very well. I never intended to hurt you, but now I can see that my words were way out of line. I'm sorry that I was so insensitive.*

♥ *I am sorry that I violated your trust. I've created a road-block in our relationship that I want to remove. I understand that even after I apologize, it may take awhile for you to venture down the road of trust with me again.*

♥ *You were promised a service that we have not provided. I am sorry that our company clearly dropped the ball this time.*

The FIVE LANGUAGES *of* APOLOGY

EXPRESSING REGRET
"I am sorry"

ACCEPTING RESPONSIBILITY
"I was wrong"

MAKING RESTITUTION
"What can I do to make it right?"

GENUINELY REPENTING
"I'll try not to do that again"

REQUESTING FORGIVENESS
"Will you please forgive me?"

3

APOLOGY LANGUAGE #2

Accepting **RESPONSIBILITY**

As a boss, Larry usually stayed calm, but on this particular day he ran out of patience. He spoke harshly to one of his employees. The message was true and the reproof needed, but he had spoken in anger and his words had been cutting. Afterward, he felt bad but told himself, *What I said was true, and the guy needs to shape up. He needs to know I'm not a pushover.*

Jane had trouble remembering appointments, especially those that fell on the weekend, when she often failed to look at her calendar. So here she was again arriving halfway through a neighborhood planning meeting. Jane's mind ran through lists of reasons for her confusion about the meeting time. At the top of the list was her recent return from a cross-country trip. She didn't know what day it was, much less the time of the day. Meanwhile, the others at the meeting felt she owed them an apology for again showing up late.

Young Shawn was in pain following a medical procedure. His mom was hovering, trying to make him comfortable and insisting that he take his pain medication. Unfortunately, Shawn swatted away his innocent mother. Shawn knew that his action was unkind and degrading, but he reasoned, *Medicine can make anyone act crazy. My mom should understand.*

Three different scenarios: unkind words, failure to come through, and lashing out. Larry, Jane, and Shawn all felt a tug of guilt. However, their excuses, they felt, covered their need to apologize.

Such actions have fractured relationships. A simple apology could make a world of difference—but an apology means accepting responsibility for one's actions.

Why is it so difficult for some of us to say, "I was wrong"? Often our reluctance to admit wrongdoing is tied to our sense of self-worth. To admit that we are wrong is perceived as weakness. We may reason, *Only losers confess. Intelligent people try to show that their actions were justified.*

The seeds of this self-justifying tendency are often planted in childhood. When a child is overly punished, condemned, or shamed for minor offenses, the sense of self-worth is diminished. Subconsciously, the child makes the emotional link between wrong behavior and low self-worth. Thus, to admit wrong is to be "bad." The child who grows up with this emotional pattern will have difficulty admitting wrongdoing as an adult because to do so strikes at his or her self-esteem.

The good news is that as adults we can understand these negative emotional patterns and yet not be imprisoned by them. The reality is that all of us are sinners; there are no perfect adults. Mature adults learn how to break the harmful patterns of childhood and accept responsibility for their own failures. The immature adult is forever rationalizing his own bad behavior.

'IT'S NOT MY FAULT'

Such rationalization often takes the form of blaming others. We may admit that what we did or said was not the best, but our behavior was provoked by the other person's irresponsible actions. Thus, we blame others and find it difficult to admit, "I was wrong." Such blaming is also a sign of immaturity. Children by nature blame others for their negative behavior. I (Gary) remember a time when my six-year-old son, confronted with knocking a glass off the table that now lay shattered on the floor, explained, "It did it by itself." To this day, my wife and I will jokingly say to each other when confronted with an irresponsible action, "It did it by itself." We both know that we are joking, but it feels so good to place the blame on "it" rather than "me."

Mature adults learn to accept responsibility for their behavior, whereas immature adults continue with childish fantasies and tend to blame others for their mistakes.

At the heart of accepting responsibility for one's behavior is the willingness to admit, "I was wrong." Paul J. Meyer, founder of Success Motivation, Inc., and coauthor of *Chicken Soup for the Golden Soul*, said, "One of the most important success factors is the willingness to admit that you were wrong."[1] I agree with Spencer Johnson, M.D., who said, "Few things are more powerful than having the common sense, wisdom, and strength to admit when you've made a mistake and to set things right."[2] Learning to say "I was wrong" is a major step toward becoming a responsible and successful adult.

OPRAH'S APOLOGY

Talk-show host Oprah Winfrey surprised her national television audience on January 26, 2006, by opening her program with these words: "I made a mistake." Winfrey was apologizing for defending an author who fictionalized many parts of his memoir, *A Million Little Pieces*. Her defense of James Frey on *Larry King Live* after Frey was found to have altered facts and misled readers alienated many of her supporters as well as book critics who found his stretching of the truth in a nonfiction work inexcusable.

Winfrey continued, "By defending Mr. Frey, I left the impression that the truth does not matter, and I am deeply sorry about that because that is not what I believe."[3] Winfrey's apology included apology language #1, *expressing regret*, as well as apology language #2, *accepting responsibility*.

By accepting responsibility for her actions, Oprah restored her respect among many who were offended. In fact, several media columnists said her willingness to respond to the concerns of her audience is what continues to make her the successful daytime host—and person—she is.[4] William Bastone, editor of *The Smoking Gun*, who had originally discovered some of the inconsistencies in Mr. Frey's book, said of Oprah's apology, "For someone like her to acknowledge that she made a mistake like that speaks really well of her. You don't often see someone of her stature admit a major mistake and apologize to her audience."[5]

Oprah's apology reminds us that even the rich and famous need to accept responsibility for their actions and express regret.

LEARNING TO ADMIT MISTAKES

In saying "I made a mistake," Winfrey was admitting she was wrong. For many individuals, hearing the words "I was wrong" is what communicates to them that the person is sincere in offering her apology. Without these or similar words that accept responsibility for one's wrong behavior, they will not sense that the other person has sincerely apologized. It doesn't matter if you are a well-known TV celebrity or a roommate in a college dormitory: Understanding this reality can make all the difference in the world when you sincerely wish to apologize for your behavior.

Joy and Rich were in my office after five years of marriage. Financially, things were going well. Rich had landed a good job upon graduating from college. Joy had worked full-time for the first two years until the baby came. Both sets of in-laws lived in town and were willing babysitters. Therefore, Rich and Joy had been able to enjoy a fair amount of leisure time together. In Joy's words: "Really, our lives are wonderful. The only problem is, Rich is never willing to apologize. When he gets upset because things don't go his way, he lashes out at me in anger. Instead of apologizing, he blames me for his anger. Even the few times he has said 'I'm sorry,' he adds 'But if you had not provoked me, I would not have gotten angry.' He excuses his behavior by shifting the blame to me. It's like he can do no wrong. He always has to put the blame on me. I know that I am not a perfect wife, but I'm willing to admit when I do wrong. Rich never admits it."

When I turned to Rich, he said, "I don't think it is right to apologize for something when it is not your fault. I do get mad, but it's because she puts me down and makes me feel like I'm not a good father. I spend as much time with our son as I can, but every week she nags me by making remarks such as 'Your son's not going to know you if you don't spend more time with him.' I have to work hard on my job, and when I get home, I'm tired. I need some time to unwind. I can't walk in the house and spend two hours playing with Ethan."

"I've never asked you to spend two hours," Joy answered. "Fifteen minutes would be a good place to start."

"That's what I'm talking about," said Rich. "If I spent fifteen minutes, I'll guarantee you she'd be asking for twenty-five the next week. I can't please her no matter what I do."

It was obvious to me that Joy's comments were striking at Rich's self-esteem. He wanted to be a good father, and her comments suggested that he was a failure. He was unwilling to accept that conclusion, and his way of expressing his hurt was to lash out with angry words. The fact is both Joy and Rich needed to apologize. The problem was that neither thought that he or she had done anything wrong.

When a relationship is fractured by hurt and anger, an apology is always in order. In this case, both Rich and Joy were hurt and angry. He was hurt by the condemning message that he heard from Joy. She was hurt by the words that Rich hurled back at her. Neither of them intended to hurt the other. Yet both of them were guilty of treating each other unkindly.

At the end of our first counseling session, I asked if next week I could see Rich alone; the following week I would see Joy alone. Then, at our fourth session, it would be the three of us together again. They agreed. I had the sense that the only satisfaction that they felt at the end of our session was that they had shared their problem with a third party and that perhaps in the weeks ahead, we might find some solutions.

Rich's Reasons

In my session with Rich, it didn't take long to discover why Joy's comments about his needing to spend more time with Ethan had provoked such a negative reaction inside him. He grew up in a home where his father was gone most of the time. Usually he left the house on Sunday evenings and returned Friday afternoons. The weekends were spent golfing and/or watching sports events. Rich had played golf with his father a few times in high school, and occasionally they watched a football game together. But Rich went off to college with a feeling that he really didn't know his father. He vowed that would never happen if he had a child; that he would find a way to connect; that his son would know that he was loved. Because of his deep desire to be a successful father, Joy's condemning words hurt deeply.

Rich's angry response followed the model he had observed in his mother, who often lashed out with angry words toward his father. Rich identified with his mother's pain and felt that she was justified in her treatment of his dad. He never blamed his mother, but often wondered why she put up with his father's behavior. Now as an adult, he felt justified in the harsh but true words he spoke to Joy. So he felt no need to apologize by acknowledging that his harsh words were wrong.

My approach was twofold. First, I tried to help Rich understand that the parental example with which he had grown up was not necessarily a healthy model. He readily agreed that his father and mother did not have the loving, caring, supportive marriage he desired. I told him that as long as he followed his parents' model, such a marriage would remain an ideal—not a reality. Second, I tried to help him see the difference between *understanding* why we do what we do and *accepting* what we do. It was easy to understand why Rich responded the way he did to Joy. But to accept that behavior as appropriate was to destroy the very thing he wanted: an intimate marriage.

The Agree/Disagree Approach

I challenged him to a new approach. It is an approach that has helped many couples live successfully in the world of human failure. I call it "agree/disagree." I *agree* that I have a right to feel hurt, angry, disappointed, and frustrated or whatever else I may be feeling. I don't choose my feelings; I simply experience them. On the other hand, I *disagree* with the idea that because of my feelings, I have the right to hurt someone else with my words or behavior. To hurt my spouse because my spouse has hurt me is like declaring civil war, a war in which there are no winners.

Therefore, I will seek to express my emotions in a way that will not be hurtful to my spouse but will hold potential for reconciliation. We worked together on a statement that Rich might deliver that would accomplish this objective. Here's what we came up with:

"Honey, I love you very much and I love Ethan very much. I want more than anything to be a good husband and a good father. Maybe I want it even more because I didn't have a close relationship with my dad, and I saw my folks fight each other all the time. Therefore, I want to share something with you that hurts me very deeply, and I want to ask you to help me find a solution. When I heard you say last night, 'If you don't spend more time with Ethan, he's going to grow up and not know who you are,' I felt a dagger pierce my heart. In fact, I went up to the computer room and cried because that's the last thing in the world I want to happen. So can you help me work on my schedule so that I can have meaningful time with Ethan and yet be able to work and meet our financial needs?"

I assured Rich that I believed that Joy would respond positively to such a statement. He agreed.

Then I said, "I've worked with people long enough to know that simply having a new plan will not necessarily stop the old patterns. Chances are sometime within the next few weeks, you will revert to your old pattern of lashing out with angry words to Joy when she makes a comment to you. It's not what you want to do, but you will do it before you think. This is when an apology is necessary. I think you will agree that yelling at one's wife is not kind, loving, tender, or positive." Rich was nodding his head. "Therefore, it is wrong."

I reminded him that the New Testament Scriptures challenge husbands to love their wives and care for them; seeking to meet their needs as Christ did for the church.[6]

"Screaming at a wife does not fit the formula for a successful marriage." Rich was nodding again. "Therefore, I want you to learn to say the words, 'Last night, I lost my temper. I yelled at you and said some pretty nasty things. I was wrong to do that. It was not tender, it was not loving, and it was not kind. I know I hurt you very much and I'm sorry, because I don't want to hurt you. And I want to ask you to forgive me. I know I was wrong.'"

Rich wrote the words down in his Palm Pilot. We prayed together and asked God's help as Rich sought to implement his new approach for handling hurt and anger. It was a heavy session, but I felt that Rich was open to change.

Joy's Challenge to Forgive

My session with Joy was more difficult—not because she didn't want to have a better marriage, but because she found it almost impossible to understand how a man could rage at his wife in anger if he really loved her. To her the two were incompatible. Therefore, she had come to question Rich's love for her.

I expressed empathy for her perspective but tried to help her understand that all of us are imperfect lovers. It is true that perfect love would never hurt the one loved. But none of us is capable of perfect love for one simple reason: We are imperfect. The Bible makes this very clear. We are all sinners.[7] Even those who say they are Christians are still capable of sinning. That is why we must learn to confess our sins to God and to the person we've sinned against.[8] Good marriages are not dependent upon perfection, but they are dependent upon a willingness to acknowledge our wrong and to seek forgiveness.

I could tell that Joy theoretically agreed with what I was saying. She had been brought up in the church, and she knew these realities. But the emotional pain that she had felt from Rich's harsh words made it very difficult for her to forgive him. "Especially when he never apologizes," she said. I agreed with her that an apology was an integral part of forgiveness and reconciliation. I asked her what she expected to hear in a genuine apology. "I want it to be sincere," she said. "I don't want him to just say 'I'm sorry that you got hurt.' I want him to acknowledge that what he did was wrong. It hurts so badly," she said. "How can he just walk away and never apologize? How could he not realize how wrong it is to scream at someone?"

For the next thirty minutes Joy and I talked about the relationship between hurt and self-esteem. I tried to explain to her the emotional dynamics of Rich's family and why her comments about his not being a good father hurt him so deeply. They may have been true at least from her perspective, but to him, it was like a verbal bomb exploding in his soul. His natural response was to fight back just as he had often seen his mother do.

"But can he change, having grown up with this model?" she asked.

"That's the wonderful thing about being human," I said. "We are capable of change, especially when we reach out for God's help. I believe that Rich is sincere, and I believe that he is beginning to understand himself better. I also believe that you will see significant change in the future," I said.

"I hope so," replied Joy. "I love him so much, and I want us to have a good marriage. I know we are in real trouble. I just hope it is not too late."

We ended our session talking about how Joy might express her own concerns about Rich's spending time with Ethan in a positive way that would not strike at his self-esteem. I suggested that if she would make a specific request of Rich, it would less likely be taken as condemnation. A suggestion or a request is very different from a demand. We explored the kind of things she might request of Rich. Here's part of the list that we came up with.

- "Would you play Chutes and Ladders with Ethan while I finish getting the meal together?"
- "Could the three of us take a walk after dinner?"
- "Would you mind giving Ethan his bath tonight?"
- "Could you read Ethan a story while I run his bathwater?"
- "Could you play with Ethan in the sandbox for a few minutes after dinner tonight while I do the dishes?"

I could see that Joy was getting the idea of specific requests rather than general complaints. I challenged her, "Never more than one request per week, OK? And when he does things with Ethan, always give him an affirming word. Tell him how proud you are of the good job he is doing as a father. Tell him how much you appreciate him playing with Ethan while you finish the meal. Don't let anything go unnoticed or unaffirmed. Since Rich wants desperately to be a good father, when you affirm him, you are building his self-esteem. And you are creating a positive emotional climate between the two of you."

Learning New Ways to Respond

The next four sessions with Rich and Joy were fully as productive as the first three. It was exciting to see them gain new insights about themselves, recognize their past emotional patterns, and develop new ways of responding to each other. Rich learned to say "I was wrong" when, on occasion, he spoke harshly to Joy. And she learned to say "I was wrong and I'm sorry I hurt you" when she would slip and make a negative comment about his skills as a father.

It became obvious in the course of our counseling that Rich's primary apology language was "I'm sorry." When Joy said these words, he was ready to forgive her. On the other hand, Joy's primary apology language was "I was wrong." What she wanted to sense was that Rich knew that his harsh words were wrong. Their marriage took a giant step forward when she learned to express genuine regret, and he learned to accept responsibility for his wrong behavior; and they learned to verbalize it to each other.

THE POWER OF APOLOGY LANGUAGE #2

For many individuals, the most important part of an apology is acknowledging that one's behavior is wrong. Linda from Seattle said to me, "My husband will not admit that he ever does anything wrong. He just sweeps it under the rug and doesn't want to talk about it anymore. If I bring it up again, he will say, 'I don't know what I did. Why can't you just forget it?' If he could admit that it was wrong, I would be willing to forgive him. But when he acts like he did nothing wrong, it's terribly difficult to overlook it."

As tears came to her eyes, she said, "I just wish I could hear him say one time 'I was wrong.'"

Pam is twenty-seven. While growing up, her dad told her that a wise person is willing to accept responsibility for his or her mistakes. "I'll never forget what he said, 'All of us make mistakes, but the only mistake that will destroy you is the one you are unwilling to admit.'

Apology Language #2: Accepting Responsibility

"I remember when I was young and would do something against the rules. He would look at me and ask, 'Do you have something you'd like to say?' He would smile and I would say, 'I made a mistake. I was wrong. Will you forgive me?' He would give me a big hug and say, 'You are forgiven.'

"Admitting my mistakes is a part of who I am, and I owe it to my father."

Five years ago Pam married Robert, whom she describes as "the most honest man I've ever met." She adds, "I don't mean he's perfect; I mean he is always willing to admit his failures.

"I guess that's why I love Robert so much, because he has always been willing to say, 'I made a mistake. I was wrong. Will you forgive me?' I like a person who is willing to accept responsibility for his mistakes."

Obviously Pam's primary apology language is accepting responsibility for one's behavior.

Michael, a twenty-four-year-old single, never heard his father apologize to his mother or to him. At eighteen he left home and has never returned to visit.

"I felt that my father was hypocritical," he explained. "In the community he was recognized as a successful man, but in my mind he was a hypocrite. I guess that's why I have always been quick to apologize, willing to admit my failures. I want my relationships to be genuine, and I know that can't happen if I'm not willing to admit that I was wrong."

Larry and Jill have been married twenty-five years. What he looks for in an apology is the admission of wrong. "A few years ago," he said, "Jill spent a lot of money from a fund given to us from one of her uncles. I felt the money should be used for our family, but she felt it was a gift and should be spent as she pleased. The money disappeared over a period of time, and I felt resentment toward her. I never spoke harshly to her, but I did tell her how I felt."

One day Jill came to him with an apology: "I realize that the way I handled the funds from Uncle Ernie was not right. I should have consulted you and allowed you to be a part of deciding how we used those funds. I was very selfish, and I realize that it hurt our relationship. I feel bad about what I've done. I know I was wrong."

Larry's response? "I accepted her apology and forgave her. It was something that could not be reversed; the money was spent, and it was time to speak of the present and not the past. I told her that I loved her and that I would not hold it against her. We held each other and cried. It was a healing time in our relationship.

"She told me later that she feared that I would be furious and hold it against her forever," Larry added. "But why should I do that when she sincerely apologized?"

For Larry, sincerity meant accepting responsibility for one's actions.

For these individuals and many others, hearing the apology language of accepting responsibility for one's wrong behavior is the most important part of an apology. It is what convinces these individuals that the apology is sincere. As one lady said, "'I'm sorry' is not enough. I want to know that he understands that what he did was wrong." For these individuals, if you want them to sense the sincerity of your apology, you might use statements such as those on the following page.

STATEMENTS OF ACCEPTING RESPONSIBILITY

♥ *I know that what I did was wrong. I could try to excuse myself, but there is no excuse. Pure and simple, what I did was selfish and wrong.*

♥ *I made a big mistake. At the time, I didn't think much about what I was doing. But in retrospect, I guess that's the problem. I wish I had thought before I acted. What I did was wrong.*

♥ *The way I spoke to you was wrong. It was harsh and untrue. I spoke out of anger, trying to justify myself. The way I talked to you was unkind and unloving. I hope you will forgive me.*

♥ *I repeated a mistake that we've discussed before. I really messed up. I know that it was my fault.*

The FIVE LANGUAGES
of APOLOGY

EXPRESSING REGRET
"I am sorry"

ACCEPTING RESPONSIBILITY
"I was wrong"

MAKING RESTITUTION
"What can I do to make it right?"

GENUINELY REPENTING
"I'll try not to do that again"

REQUESTING FORGIVENESS
"Will you please forgive me?"

4

APOLOGY LANGUAGE #3

Making RESTITUTION

T he idea of "making things right" to make up for a wrong is embedded within the human psyche, and both our judicial system and our human relationships are deeply influenced by this fundamental idea. In recent years, the American judicial system has given more emphasis to what is legally called *reparative damages*: the concept that the criminal should repay his victim for the damages incurred by the criminal's behavior. Rather than simply spending time in prison, the criminal needs to make efforts to make up for the wrong to the one who was wronged.

The idea of reparative damages is based on the innate human sense that when a wrong has been committed, it should be "paid for." Traditionally we have said of those in prison, "They are paying their debt to society." The idea of reparative damages takes it one step further and says, "You need to pay your debt to the person you wronged."

In some cases, this is fairly easy to do. If the crime has involved something of monetary value, then the criminal can repay the cost of the damages. In other situations, however, it is more difficult. When the crime is rape or murder, how could the killer or rapist repay the victim or the surviving family members? "Reparations" in these cases could include, for example, the criminal sincerely apologizing to the parties involved, acknowledging his wrongdoing, and committing the rest of his life to helping young people—and keeping them from following in his footsteps.

Since criminals normally do not take initiative to seek to repay their victims, our legal system is overrun with cases in which people are seeking restitution for the damages they incur at the hands of another. Something deep within the human psyche says, "If I have been wronged, someone needs to pay." Parents seek to teach children this principle. When a mother sees a four-year-old son grab a doll from the hands of his six-year-old sister, the mother requires him not only to say "I'm sorry" but to also return the doll.

'I OUGHT TO DO SOMETHING TO MAKE AMENDS'

The *New Webster's Dictionary* defines *restitution* as "the act of giving back to a rightful owner" or "a giving of something as an equivalent for what has been lost, damaged, etc." In his book *Since Nobody's Perfect . . . How Good Is Good Enough?* Andy Stanley writes, "A willingness to do something to try to make up for the pain I have caused you is evidence of a true apology. A voice inside us says, 'I ought to do something to make amends for what I have done.'"[1]

Everett Worthington Jr., professor of psychology at Virginia Commonwealth University and a leader in research on forgiveness, calls the act of making such amends "equalizing."

> Equalizing is making up for the loss that the other person experienced. To offer restitution is to equalize the balance of justice. Any hurt or offense causes the person who is hurt to lose something. Perhaps he or she loses self-esteem, self-respect, or a tangible benefit (such as if I

offend you in front of your boss and you lose a promotion opportunity).
So it is an act of kindness for the transgressor to offer to make up for
the loss.[2]

'DO YOU STILL LOVE ME?'

In the public arena, our emphasis upon restitution is based upon our
sense of justice. The one who commits the crime should pay for the
wrongdoing. In contrast, in the private sphere of family and other
close relationships, our desire for restitution is almost always based
upon our need for love. After being hurt deeply, we need the reassurance that the person who hurt us still loves us. After all, successful
family relationships and true friendships are ultimately based on love.

It is true that when we are hurt by the words or behavior of a family member, we often feel angry. The reason it hurts so deeply and the
reason the anger is so intense is that we desperately want to be loved
by that person. Their harsh words or hurtful actions have called into
question their love.

"How could they love me and do that?" is the question that lingers
in our minds. The words "I'm sorry; I was wrong" may not be enough.
We want to know the answer to the question, "Do you still love me?"
It is the answer to this question that requires restitution.

For some people, restitution is their primary apology language.
For them the statement, "It is not right for me to have treated you that
way," must be followed with "What can I do to show you that I still
care about you?" Without this effort at restitution, this person will
question the sincerity of the apology. They will continue to feel
unloved even though you may have said, "I am sorry; I was wrong."
They wait for the reassurance that you genuinely love them.

MAKING THINGS RIGHT

This reality surfaced again and again in our research. Over and over
again people made statements such as the following:

"I expect some sense of contrition but also a sincere effort to amend the damage caused by the rift."

"I expect him to try to repair what has gone wrong."

"I expect her to be truly sorry from the heart and be willing to make things right."

"I want him to make amends as appropriate. Things don't just go away by saying 'I'm sorry.'"

All of these individuals viewed the effort to make restitution as the strongest evidence of the sincerity of the apology. Their primary apology language is restitution.

Returning to our discussion of prison, if someone broke a law, he or she might be assigned to community service as a form of restitution. In relationships, you might perform acts of service to benefit your relationship.

The question, then, is how do we make restitution in the most effective way? Since the heart of restitution is reassuring the spouse or family member that you genuinely love him or her, it is essential to express restitution in the love language of the other person. Some husbands have the idea that the best way to express restitution is by flowers. "Give her flowers and everything will be all right" is their perception. However, the gift of flowers is not the love language of all women. That's why some husbands have had their flowers pushed back into their faces, while the wife walks away in disgust, saying, "He thinks flowers solve everything!"

LEARNING THE FIVE LOVE LANGUAGES

After thirty-five years of marriage and family counseling, I am convinced that there are fundamentally five emotional love languages. Each person has one of the five as a primary language. If you speak his/her primary love language, he/she will be reassured of your love, and restitution will be successful. However, if you don't speak the primary love language, your best efforts at apologizing may not be successful. Therefore, let me review briefly the five love languages[3] and illustrate from my research how speaking the primary love language will make your efforts at restitution successful.

Words of Affirmation

Love language number one is *words of affirmation*, using words to affirm the other person. "You look nice in that outfit"; "I really appreciate what you did for me"; "You are so thoughtful"; "Every day I am reminded of how much I love you"; "I really appreciate this meal. You are an excellent cook. I know it takes a lot of time and energy, and I really appreciate it." Using words to affirm the other person may focus on his/her personality, behavior, dress, accomplishments, or beauty. The important thing is that words communicate verbally your affection and appreciation for the person.

Here are a couple of examples from our research of people for whom words of affirmation is their primary love language and how hearing those words made their spouse's efforts at restitution successful.

Megan is twenty-nine and has been married to Brad for six years. "I know that Brad's apology is sincere when he retracts his hurtful words and then tells me how much he loves me. Sometimes he goes to the extreme in telling me how wonderful I am and how sorry he is that he hurt me. I guess he knows that it takes a lot of positive words to make up for the hurtful things he has said."

Tim met with me during a break at one of my marriage seminars. We had been discussing apologies, and he said of his wife, "She's almost always successful in her apologies. She's the best apologizer I know."

I was impressed, and listened intently as he explained. "She generally says something like, 'Tim, I am so sorry that I . . . You are so wonderful and I'm so sorry that I've hurt you. Will you please forgive me?' And then she gives me a hug. It works every time. It's those words 'You are so wonderful' that get me. I've never failed to forgive her because I know she's sincere. We all make mistakes; I don't expect her to be perfect. But it surely feels good when she tells me how wonderful I am while asking me to forgive her."

For Tim, words of affirmation reflect his primary love language and that's his favorite part of an apology. It's all the restitution he needs.

Acts of Service

A second love language is *acts of service*. This love language is based on the old axiom "Actions speak louder than words." For these people, love is demonstrated by thoughtful acts of kindness. Vacuuming a floor, washing dishes, changing the baby's diaper, getting bugs off the windshield, taking the garbage outside, doing the laundry, washing the dog, and helping the children with their homework are all acts of service. For those individuals for whom this is their primary love language, nothing reassures them of your love like acts of service.

Gwen was in my office, and she was visibly upset. "I'm sick and tired of his apologies," she said. "'I'm sorry, I'm sorry, I'm sorry.' That's all he ever says. That's supposed to make everything all right. Well, *I'm* sorry, but when he screams and yells at me and calls me names, that doesn't make it all right.

"What I want to know is: Does he still love me, or does he want out of the marriage? If he loves me, then why doesn't he do something to help me around the house? I'm tired of living with a man who sits in front of the TV while I cook the meals and wash the dishes. I work outside the home as well as he. He doesn't even keep the grass mowed. How can he love me and do nothing? Actions speak louder than words."

Obviously, Gwen's primary love language is acts of service, and her husband is not speaking it. Therefore, his apologies fall on deaf ears. She cannot conceive that he could be sincerely sorry and yet fail to love her.

I spent some time with Gwen and explained to her the five love languages and told her that my guess was that her husband had no clue as to what her love language was. And she probably had no idea about his love language. Within three months she and her husband, Mark, had discovered—and were speaking—each other's primary love language. Their marriage was back on track too. He realized that a verbal apology to her was never enough. It had to involve restitution—the reassurance of his love—and this needed to be expressed in acts of service. I don't see Mark often, but when I do, he always thanks me for the insights on love and apology that "saved my marriage."

At the conclusion of my marriage seminars, I typically invite the husband to take his wife's hands, look into her eyes, and repeat after me the following words: "I know I'm not a perfect husband. I hope you will forgive me for past failures. I sincerely want to be a better husband, and I'm asking you to teach me how." Then I ask the wives to repeat similar words to the husbands. One woman, unable to say those words to her husband, later revealed on one of our apology research questionnaires that she could not think of one time her husband made a successful apology during their thirteen-year marriage. But then she added, "My first hope [of having him truly apologize] was at the end of your conference. I couldn't say the words back to him at that moment, but by that evening, he was helping with the kids and with dinner. I knew that something had happened to him. I'm hoping he has discovered that acts of service is my love language."

"It remains to be seen if he will continue this change of behavior," she continued, admitting her doubts. "I know that if I felt like he really loved me, I would be willing to forgive him for everything in the past. More than anything, I want my husband to love me." The success of his apology is now dependent upon him making amends for the past by reassuring his wife that he loves her by speaking her primary love language.

This same principle applies in friendships. Ben was a handsome, intelligent city planner, who ran into a conflict with Steve, another planner in his work group. Initially, Ben and Steve felt that they had a lot in common, and they had enjoyed discussing their shared interests in golf and politics over lunch most days. One day, as a practical joke, Steve commandeered Ben's office computer while Ben was away. Steve pretended to be Ben and sent out an e-mail to their six-person work group, inviting them all to come to Ben's house for a New Year's Eve dinner party: "Don't bring a thing—just yourself!" The next day, a colleague alerted Ben about the counterfeit invitation. Far from being amused, Ben felt angry and betrayed.

When confronted by Ben, Steve could tell that Ben really hadn't appreciated the joke, and he offered a sincere apology. Before Ben could accept the apology, however, he needed Steve to make things right. At Ben's insistence, Steve sent out a correction e-mail to the work group. This retraction allowed Ben to feel that Steve had owned up to the problem he had created and set things right again. Their friendship had a second chance. Had Steve been unwilling to take this action, Ben would have considered his apology incomplete, likely ending their friendship.

Receiving Gifts

A third love language is *receiving gifts*. It is universal to give and receive gifts as an expression of love. Anthropologists have explored the ethnographies of hundreds of cultures around the world. They have never discovered a culture where gift giving is not an expression of love. A gift says, "He was thinking about me. Look what he got for me."

The gifts need not be expensive. Haven't people always said, "It's the thought that counts"? However, it is not the thought left in your head that counts but rather the gift that came out of the thought in your head.

From an early age, children will pick dandelions from the front yard and give them as expressions of love to their mothers. Wives and husbands can do the same thing, though I wouldn't suggest dandelions. Even as an adult, you don't have to pay much: If you have no flowers in your yard, try your neighbor's yard. Ask them; they will give you a flower.

For some people, receiving gifts is their primary love language. Therefore, if the person you've offended prefers the love language of *receiving gifts* and you wish to make amends for the wrong you have done, giving gifts will be an effective method of restitution.

Bethany finds her husband's apologies sincere, because he speaks her language. "He makes his apology; then that evening, he brings me a rose to make up for what he has done that has offended me. I don't know what it is, but the rose seems to communicate to me that he is really sincere. So I forgive him."

"How many roses have you received through the years?" I asked.

"Dozens," she answered. "But every time I receive one, it says to me that he still loves me." For her, the gift was restitution.

With their son sick with leukemia and often in the hospital, Susan tried to understand her husband's tenseness. "A lot of pain and anger was taken out on me, but I let it slide off because I understood. Out of the blue one day, he walked into the hospital room with flowers and a card and a full apology for taking his stress out on me. It was one of the most tender times in our marriage. He realized by his own conviction that he was hurting me, and he took the initiative to apologize. The flowers and the card sealed it for me. I knew he was sincere."

He not only apologized, but he made restitution by speaking Susan's love language, *receiving gifts*.

Quality Time

Love language number four is *quality time*. Giving another person your undivided attention communicates, "You are important to me." Quality time means no distractions. The TV is off; the magazine is on the table along with the book. You are not paying the bills; you are not looking at a computer screen. You are giving the other person your undivided attention. If I give my wife twenty minutes of quality time,

I have given her twenty minutes of my life, and she has done the same for me. It is a powerful emotional communicator of love.

For some people, this is their primary love language. Nothing communicates love more deeply than quality time. Such times do not even need to include major activities or projects together; they can simply be extended conversations between two individuals. For those individuals, quality time is an excellent way to make restitution.

Mary from St. Louis recalls a powerful apology she received the Sunday afternoon after attending the marriage conference. She and her husband had lunch together, and they were beginning to relax when "Phil looked at me and said how sorry he was for how he had been treating me. He was just miserable, and we weren't even talking to each other.

"He looked at me while holding my hands and thanked me for buying the tickets for the conference. He told me that it had opened his eyes and challenged him to be the husband he had neglected to be for the past five years of our marriage.

"Just seeing the true joy and sorrow in his eyes convinced me that he was sincere. The fact that he set aside time to talk to me and to apologize for his actions the past week was almost more than I could believe. In the past every time he tried to apologize, he would say 'I'm sorry,' and that was it. It was like putting catsup on a hotdog; just something you always do. But this time, it was different. I knew that he was sincere, and I freely forgave him."

Phil was speaking Mary's love language, quality time, and that made all the difference.

You don't have to hold hands, but you do need to give your full attention to the person to whom you are apologizing. If the person you've offended feels loved by having quality time with you, then only quality time will convince them that your apology is sincere. Giving your undivided attention while making the apology is restitution enough. It communicates deeply to the person that he or she is loved.

Physical Touch

Love language number five is *physical touch*. We have long known the emotional power of physical touch. That's why we pick up babies and hold and cuddle them. Long before they understand the meaning of the word *love*, they feel loved by physical touch. The same is true of adults. Holding hands, kissing, embracing, putting an arm around the shoulder, giving a pat on the back, or running your hand through their hair are all expressions of the language of physical touch. We're not talking just husbands and wives. Physical touch is appropriate among all family members, including mothers and sons and fathers and daughters.

For some individuals, this is their primary love language. Nothing speaks more deeply of love than affirming touch. For them, an apology without touch will appear insincere.

Robert and his ten-year-old, Jake, had gotten into an argument. In the heat of anger, Robert had accused his son of being lazy and irresponsible. Jake began crying uncontrollably. Robert knew that his words had been extremely hurtful to Jake.

"I'm sorry," he said. "I lost my temper. What I said is wrong. You are not lazy, and you are not irresponsible. You are a ten-year-old boy who loves to play and enjoy life. I should have been more thoughtful about asking you to interrupt your game to do something that I wanted you to do. I love you very much, and it hurts me to know that I have hurt you."

He walked over to Jake, put his arms around him, and gave him a big bear hug. Jake sobbed even more uncontrollably, but this time with great relief. When he gained his composure, his father looked him in the eyes and said, "I love you so much." And Jake said, "I love you too, Dad," as he gave his father a hug around the neck. His father's apology was effective because he made restitution by speaking his son's primary love language, physical touch.

"What do you expect in an apology from your wife?" we asked Judson from Minneapolis, who had been married to his wife for fifteen years. He responded, "I expect her to understand that what she did was very hurtful, say that she is sorry, and then ask for my forgiveness. After granting forgiveness, there has to be a hug for the apology process to be complete."

Judson is clearly revealing that he expects restitution to be a part of the apology process, and physical touch is the language of love which he understands best. After the hug, he feels that she has "made amends" for her wrong. Without the hug, the apology process is lacking something important for him.

Marti's illustration of a successful apology indicated how important physical touch was to her. "My husband made a hurtful remark to me in front of the children. At the time, I reacted and he defended his words. Some days later when we were all at the table, he stood behind me, put his hands on my shoulders, and said in front of our three children that what he had done was wrong and he was sorry and that he wanted to acknowledge it to me and to those who had witnessed it. His apology worked because 1) he admitted he was wrong, 2) he brought healing through his touch, 3) he made his apology public to all who were involved, which made me admire him for teaching his children an important lesson, and 4) for restoring my reputation." The words were important, but it was the affirming touch that "brought healing" and assured her of her husband's love.

If physical touch is one's primary love language, and I want to make a sincere apology, then I must communicate restitution by reaching out to give affirming touches. Words alone will not suffice. It is the touch that makes amends for the wrongs.

WHEN THE MESSAGE ISN'T GETTING THROUGH

In making restitution, one size does not fit all. That is why many husbands and wives have been frustrated in their efforts to "make it right." It seemed that no matter what they did, they could not do enough. The problem is they were not speaking their spouse's primary love language.

Therefore, the message of restitution—reaffirming love—was not getting through. Effective restitution requires learning the love language of your loved one and speaking it as a part of your apology.

If restitution is the primary apology language of an individual, then this becomes the most important part of the apology. "I'm sorry; I was wrong" will never be taken as sincere if these words are not accompanied by a sincere effort at restitution. They wait for the assurance that you still genuinely love them. Without your effort to make amends, the apology will not have the desired results of forgiveness and reconciliation.

REPAYING AND RESTORING

Restitution often extends beyond expressing love through speaking one of the five languages of love. It may require *repayment* or *restoring* of something taken—a damaged car, a scratched watch . . . or even a good name. Remember, Marti's good name was restored when Jim publicly acknowledged his "hurtful comment" had taken away his wife's good name among their children. The desire to make amends for one's wrong behavior is a natural part of apologizing if one is indeed sincere.

A Tax Collector Makes Amends

There is a fascinating story recorded in the life of Jesus. The great teacher was passing through the town of Jericho. His fame had preceded Him. In that town lived a tax collector named Zacchaeus. Tax collectors were not the most popular people among the ordinary Jewish populace because they often charged exorbitant taxes for their Roman bosses and pocketed great profit. Zacchaeus wanted to see and hear Jesus, the prophet about whom he had heard so much.

A rather short man, Zacchaeus had a clever strategy. He planned to climb a tree and look down upon Jesus. There he could see and hear, yet go unnoticed by the crowd. However, when Jesus came to the tree, He looked up and said to Zacchaeus, "Come down. I'd like to go to your house for dinner." Zacchaeus was shocked and deeply moved. Apparently he recognized that he was dealing with a man who knew of his self-centered lifestyle and yet was willing to associate with him.

Immediately, Zacchaeus apologized for his wrong behavior through the years and then said that he planned to repay all those from whom he had taken funds unjustly. In fact, he promised to repay them four times as much as he had taken. Jesus interpreted this as the sign of a genuine confession, and He even held up Zacchaeus as an example of how to deal with failure.[4]

When Nations Apologize

In recent decades, entire nations have apologized to entire people groups for wrongs done them by the national government, and many have included restitution in the form of paying reparations. The American government has apologized several times to Japanese-American victims and during one of these apologies included payment of $20,000 to each survivor. Germany's many statements have included apologies to German Jews, Polish Jews, and other Jewish victims of the Holocaust, and have included reparations.

Within the United States, the issue of a national apology is especially pertinent to the African-American community because of the evil system of slavery, which was legal until 1865. Both the government and corporate America continue to discuss the complex issue of apologizing for slavery, weighing various proposals on how best to make restitution to the descendants of those African-Americans who were enslaved.

A genuine apology will be accompanied by a desire to right the wrongs committed, to make amends for the damage done, and to assure the person that you genuinely care about him or her. If you are not certain what the offended person might consider proper restitution, you might ask questions like the following:

STATEMENTS OF RESTITUTION

♥ *Is there anything I can do to make up for what I have done?*

♥ *I know I have hurt you deeply, and I feel like I should do something to repay you for the hurt I've caused. Can you give me a suggestion?*

♥ *I don't feel right just saying "I'm sorry." I want to make up for what I've done. What would you consider appropriate?*

♥ *I know that I've inconvenienced you. May I give you some of my time to balance things out?*

♥ *I regret that I've damaged your honor. May I make a (public) correction?*

♥ *I've broken this promise a million times. Would you like for me to put my commitment to you in writing this time?*

The FIVE LANGUAGES of APOLOGY

EXPRESSING REGRET
"I am sorry"

ACCEPTING RESPONSIBILITY
"I was wrong"

MAKING RESTITUTION
"What can I do to make it right?"

GENUINELY REPENTING
"I'll try not to do that again"

REQUESTING FORGIVENESS
"Will you please forgive me?"

APOLOGY LANGUAGE #4

Genuinely REPENTING

We have the same old arguments about the same old things," said a wife who's been married nearly thirty years. "I think that's true of most couples. What upsets me most is not the offending action—it's the *repetition* of the offending action. He apologizes. He promises not to do it again. Then . . . he does it again— 'it' being as small as leaving the bathroom light on or as annoying as needless crabbiness.

"I don't want apologies. I want him not to do the thing that bothers me—ever!"

This woman wants her husband to repent.

The word *repentance* means "to turn around" or "to change one's mind." It is illustrated by someone who is walking west and, for whatever reason, suddenly turns 180 degrees and walks toward the east. In the context of an apology, it means that an individual realizes that his or her present behavior is destructive. The person regrets the pain he or she is causing the other person, and he chooses to change his behavior.

Repentance is more than saying, "I'm sorry; I was wrong. How can I make this up to you?" It is saying, "I'll try not to do this again." For some individuals, it is repentance that convinces them that the apology is sincere. The offending person's repentance, then, elicits the offended person's forgiveness.

Without genuine repentance, the other languages of apology may fall on deaf ears. What people who've been hurt want to know is, "Do you intend to change, or will this happen again next week?"

In our research, we asked the question, "What do you expect in an apology?" Repeatedly we heard statements like the following:

"Show that you are willing to change, and do it differently next time."

"I expect them to find ways to stop it from happening again."

"I expect a change of behavior so that the insult does not recur."

"I want them to have a plan for improvement, a plan to succeed and not to fail."

"A sincere apology should have a component of willingness not to repeat the offense."

"I expect him not to go into a rage a few minutes later or do the same thing again."

These and scores of similar statements reveal that for many people, repentance is at the heart of a true apology.

'I WANT TO CHANGE'

How then do we speak the language of repentance? *It begins with an expression of intent to change.* All true repentance begins in the heart. We recognize that what we have done is wrong, that our actions have hurt the one we love. We don't want to continue this behavior; therefore, we decide that with God's help, we will change. Then we verbalize this decision to the person we have offended. It is the decision to change that indicates that we are no longer making excuses. We are not minimizing our behavior but are accepting full responsibility for our actions.

When we share our intention to change with the person we have offended, we are communicating to them what is going on inside of us. They get a glimpse of our heart—and this often is the language that convinces them we mean what we say.

Abby is twenty-seven and thinks her husband, Bob, is a good apologizer. "What makes you think his apologies are sincere?" I asked.

"Well, he's very honest," she replied. "And what I really like is that he tells me he'll try not to let it happen again. To me this is really important. I don't want to just hear words; I want to see changes. When he indicates that he intends to change, I'm always willing to forgive him."

Jim, thirty-five, explained what he seeks in an apology. "I expect the person to come to me and sit down face-to-face, not over the phone, and tell me that they were wrong and tell me that they're going to make changes so that it won't happen again. I want them to be realistic and tell me that they know they have to work on it so I should be patient with them."

Whether it's a coworker or family member, Jim wants to see changes, although he is willing to wait for those changes. "I know that changes don't happen overnight, but admitting that you are willing to work on changing is what's important to me."

Some may resist the idea of verbally expressing an intention to change for fear that someone will not actually change. "Won't that simply make things worse?" one man asked me. It is true that changing behavior takes time, and in the process we may have additional failures. (I'll talk about that later in the chapter.) But these failures need not keep us from ultimately making genuine positive changes.

The bigger question is, "What if you fail to verbalize your intention to change?" Your philosophy may be, "Just make the changes; don't talk about them." The problem with that approach is that the offended person cannot read your mind. He or she doesn't know that in your heart you have decided to make changes. It may take weeks or months for them to observe the changes, but even then they may not know what motivated the changes. When apologizing, it is far better to state your intention to change. Then the person knows that you truly recognize that your behavior is wrong—and that you fully intend to change the behavior.

It is perfectly fine to tell them that you hope they will be patient with you because you know you will not be 100 percent successful immediately, but that it is your intention to change this destructive behavior. Now they know your intention and sense that your apology is sincere so they can now forgive you even before the changes are actually made.

'I'LL APOLOGIZE, BUT I WON'T CHANGE'

Expressing the intention to change may be difficult if you think that what you are doing is not morally wrong; your actions might offend others, but you believe that this is simply a part of who you are. Craig is by nature a joker—jovial, always making a humorous comment. The problem is that many of his jokes are off-color. This greatly offends and embarrasses his wife, Betty. Craig replies, "Hey, they aren't dirty jokes; they're jokes that everyone can identify with. That's why I get so many laughs." However, Betty is not laughing, and this joking has become a huge issue in their marriage.

Craig is willing to say, "I'm sorry I offended you. It is not my intention to hurt you." But he is not willing to say, "I was wrong, and I will change the kind of jokes I tell."

In my office, he defended himself by saying, "No one else finds my jokes offensive." With a little research, we found out that statement was untrue. A number of people, especially women in his office, found his jokes offensive. They had simply not taken the initiative to confront him.

A few weeks later when I shared this information with Craig, he began to think differently. However, it should not have taken this information for Craig to have repented of his behavior. The fact that it deeply hurt his wife and created a huge emotional barrier between the two of them should have been enough to motivate him to make changes. It was, in fact, his unwillingness to repent that had brought the marriage to the point of divorce. When Craig realized it was change or lose his marriage, he was willing to change. That was fourteen years ago. Today Craig and Betty have a strong marriage. They even lead a marriage enrichment class in their church.

The idea that we only need to make changes when we are doing something morally wrong is erroneous. In a healthy marriage, we often make changes that have nothing to do with morality but everything to do with building a harmonious marriage. For example, I don't enjoy vacuuming floors, but I do it regularly. I repented of my insensitivity to meeting Karolyn's needs when I discovered that her primary love language is acts of service, and that vacuuming floors is a special dialect which she greatly appreciates.

Vacuuming in itself is not a moral issue. It is, however, a *marital* issue and can make the difference between a wife feeling loved and not feeling loved. I much prefer to live with a wife whose love tank is full. Therefore, my repentance was a small price to pay for the privilege of living with a happy woman.

BEYOND WORDS—TO REAL CHANGE

The second step down the road of repentance is developing a plan for implementing change. Often apologies fail to be successful in restoring the relationship because there is no plan for making positive changes. Jan and Clyde recently celebrated their silver anniversary, but she admits they don't have much of a marriage after twenty-five years. "He has a drinking problem." She says, "He often apologizes for the way he treats me when he is drinking, but we both know these are merely words. Words are said in sincerity at the moment, but both of us know that there is no commitment to stand behind the words, no plan for making changes."

Checking himself into a residential treatment center is a plan that could radically change their lifestyle and marriage, but to this point Clyde has been unwilling to have a plan to change, so he continues down the same predictable road.

Another wife said, "Flowers and apologies were typical after his womanizing episodes. The problem is there were never any changes. I eventually got sick of his apologies and threw his flowers in his face. We've been divorced ten years now."

'He's a Good Man, and I Don't Want to Lose Him'

I met Rick and Rita in New Orleans after my lecture on *The Five Love Languages*. Rick began, "We're having problems in our marriage." He explained that after reading *The Five Love Languages* a year earlier, he realized his love languages are physical touch and quality time. He told this to Rita and thought her speaking his love languages would help their marriage.

"At the time, I was feeling really unloved by her," Rick said, with Rita standing at his side. "She spent all of her time with her mother and her friends. I felt like she was married to them more than she was married to me. At the time she told me she was sorry, that she did not want to hurt me, that she loved me very much, and that she would try to speak my love languages, but that was the end of it. Nothing ever changed. It was like we didn't even have the conversation.

"It's a year later, and I still feel unloved. I feel like she doesn't care about me or our marriage."

I looked at Rita, who was standing next to him. "I really do love him," she said. "It's just that I didn't grow up in a 'touchy-feely' family and I find it difficult to initiate physical touch. I enjoy spending time with him; it's just that I work full-time, my mother's very demanding, and I like to go out with the girls one evening a week and before I know it, all the time is gone."

"Would you sincerely like to have a better marriage?" I asked Rita.

"I really would," she said. "He's a good man, and I don't want to lose him." In the next five minutes I mapped out a plan for her on how to learn to speak the love language of physical touch. Then I shared some ideas about quality time. I challenged her to sit down with Rick for fifteen minutes on Monday, Wednesday, and Friday nights and discuss their day and how things went. I told her she would find other ideas on how to speak the language of quality time in the book and urged her to read that chapter again.

It was a quick conversation and one that I would have forgotten had it not been for a letter I received six months later. Rick said, "Dr. Chapman, I can't thank you enough for the time you spent with Rita and me at your seminar in New Orleans. It made all the difference in the world. Rita took your plan seriously. She has become extremely fluent in speaking my love languages. I am a happy man and I just wanted you to know that you have made a difference in our marriage." Rita made changes once she had a plan. She had the desire to meet Rick's needs much earlier, but the desire was not turned into reality until she adopted a plan for making changes. Plans need not be elaborate, but they need to be specific.

'He Was So Sincere, It Made Me Cry'

Sometimes the offended party will be able to help you work out a plan. As we were doing the research for this book, I (Jennifer) gave a lecture to a small group of women on *The Five Languages of Apology*. A few weeks later I got a call from Clara, one of the ladies who attended. She told me the following story. "My husband, Chet, is a fantastic father, but we all have our moments. One night, he strongly rebuked our four-year-old son out of his own anger and frustration. My son was pushing all of his hot buttons. My husband did not hurt our son physically, but his rage did scare him terribly. I was so upset that I told him if he ever acted that way again toward either of our children, I would leave him."

Clara and her husband had agreed they'd never threaten each other with leaving, yet she felt anger and dismay over his behavior. "I feared being forced to protect my child against his own father," she explained.

"I told Chet that I needed an apology. He said, 'I'm sorry, but . . .' and then he started talking about how our son was acting, which provoked his anger. After thirty minutes of discussion, I felt no better." So Clara mentioned what she had learned in the apology lecture and asked that they use some of those ideas. Chet then said he was sorry, but it felt insincere to Clara.

"I needed him to see how he was 100 percent wrong and responsible in disciplining out of anger. I needed him to see how it scared both our son and me." Clara wanted a plan "so that it would never happen again. I needed to know he was committed to making that plan work."

"Before I knew about the apology languages, I would have accepted his initial weak apology. I would have walked away feeling hurt and angry. A bit of intimacy would have been eaten away from our marriage. Instead, just the opposite happened. I identified what I needed and he provided it. He fully repented and admitted he was wrong."

The two worked together on a plan, and the next morning, he apologized. "He was so sincere, it made me cry. The tears released the hurt and anger in my soul, and we were actually more intimate than before. He also apologized to our son. Our son told him, 'Dad, I was really scared.' My husband's heart broke. He asked, 'Would you forgive Daddy?' My son replied, 'Yes.' Then my husband said, 'I will never do that again.'"

Clara told me that a part of the plan they worked out together was that if her husband felt himself getting angry with the children, he would go to her and say, "I'm getting heated. Will you please take over?" He would take a walk around the block and come back and try to help her in any way he could. "So far the plan is working really well," Clara said.

It is ideal when couples can help each other work out a plan to correct a behavior that is troublesome to one of them.

PUT IT IN WRITING!

The third step down the road of repentance is implementing the plan. A plan that is not implemented is like a seed that is not planted. Making the plan work requires thought and action. I (Gary) have often found it helpful to write on an index card the changes I am trying to implement and to post them on the mirror where I shave in the mornings. It is a way of keeping them on the front burner of my mind. I am more likely to make the changes if I am consciously aware of what I am trying to do differently today.

Writing it down also helps make the plan concrete and specific rather than general. For example, a general plan might be, "I will try not to blame her for my negative emotions." A more specific plan might be, "I will start my sentences with 'I' rather than 'you.'" Example: "I feel angry," rather than "You make me angry." This is a plan that you are more likely to implement, because it is specific. Following through with the plan gives evidence to the offended party that your apology was sincere.

Small Changes, Big Difference

Joel's wife, Joyce, was quarrelsome. It seemed to Joel that almost everything she said was negative, and whatever he said, she disagreed with. In our counseling sessions it became obvious to me that for Joyce the world was either black or white. She tended to see everything as good or bad, right or wrong. Thus, if she disagreed with Joel's idea, his idea was "wrong." It took awhile for her to come to understand the difference between something being morally wrong and something being simply a different way of doing or seeing things. Much of life falls into a nonmoral category. The way one paints a house, washes a car, or mows the grass is not a moral issue. It is important to find ways to disagree without being condemning.

Another reality is that people perceive things in different ways. When Joyce realized that her speech patterns came across to Joel as judgmental and that this hurt him very deeply and affected their marital relationship, she was open to exploring ways of changing her communication patterns.

One of the plans Joyce developed was that if she disagreed with Joel's idea, she would first give an affirming statement and then share her opinion. We actually wrote out three affirming statements that she might try.

1. "That's an interesting way to look at it."
2. "I can appreciate that."
3. "One of the things I like about that idea is . . ."

When sharing her opinions, Joyce agreed that she would start her sentences with, "My perception of that is . . ." Joel indicated that he thought that this plan would make a great deal of difference for him and that he would really appreciate Joyce's efforts to respect his opinions.

The following week, Joyce indicated that it had been very difficult for her to implement the plan. "I guess I've been in a rut for so long, it's difficult to change my thought and speech patterns," she said. "But by the middle of the week I was beginning to make the transition. I immediately saw how differently Joel responded. I guess it was seeing the smile on his face and knowing that he was pleased with my efforts that encouraged me to continue working."

She had written the three affirming statements on an index card and read them several times throughout the day. "The card really helped," she said, adding, "I never knew that such a small change would make such a big difference in our relationship."

Counting the Cost

Sometimes implementing the plan for change can be extremely costly. Caroline came to me (Jennifer) for counseling to help her deal with depression and feelings of betrayal. She had married an attractive, professional athlete named Chris when they were each twenty-two years old. Shortly after the birth of their first child, her husband had begun an affair with a younger woman. When confronted by Caroline about the affair, Chris admitted wrongdoing and said that he wanted to repair the marriage.

During counseling, Caroline and I discussed terms under which she would be willing to work on rebuilding the marriage. For Caroline, it was critical for her to hear from Chris that he was not only sorry for his wrong action but that he would make changes in his lifestyle.

In the end, Chris made a very drastic change. He left the professional sports world and took a desk job in order to avoid temptation. In addition, Chris worked to rebuild Caroline's trust by telling her where he would be and opening up his cell phone and e-mail accounts to his wife.

Caroline needed to know that things would be different in the future, and Chris offered these concessions in order to reestablish trust. Caroline forgave Chris, and five years later, they have a strong marriage.

"At first, I couldn't believe that Chris would make all of those changes for me. I didn't even ask him to give up his athletic career, but his actions spoke volumes to me. I have never doubted his sincerity or his commitment. I feel so loved by him," she said.

The plan may call for huge changes or minor changes; it may involve huge issues or minor details. For one special anniversary,

David tried to make arrangements to go away with Anna to a really nice place on their actual anniversary date. He booked a place, but then it was needed for a wedding reception, and the hotel wanted to relocate them. "David started out talking to me about whether or not we wanted to relocate," Anna recalls, "but then he went ahead and made other arrangements without my input. Needless to say, I was not happy."

Anna was upset not about the new location, but her husband's independent decision. Fortunately, he realized his mistake and apologized. "David caught on quickly with my not-so-pleased look and apologized for not asking what I would have liked. Then he called them back and made the arrangement we had originally decided on together, but one month after our anniversary date." Though the change of plans was not as big as Joyce's change of speaking patterns or Chris's departure from pro sports, it had the same outcome: an improved relationship.

Anna's take on David's willingness to change: "We both greatly enjoyed our time away." David demonstrated genuine repentance: He was willing to back up, think differently, and turn around and go in the other direction. It was his follow-through that made Anna aware of his sincerity.

Jane and Paula were close high school friends who decided to room together when they went off to the same college. In high school, their friendship had been close and comfortable. In college, Jane was quite social, and she busied herself with new activities. Paula, on the other hand, was more introverted, and she wished that Jane would spend more time with her in their shared dormitory room. Jane noticed that Paula rarely went out except to attend her classes. So she invited Paula to join her in attending a weekly activity with her friends as well her trips to the gym. Paula consistently refused, saying, "No, because . . ." almost before Jane finished her offer. But Paula grew increasingly resentful of Jane's rich social life.

One evening, the lid that Paula had been keeping on her resentment blew off, and in a fit of anger she accused Jane of being a cold, uncaring, self-centered, unavailable, terrible friend and roommate. Jane was quite hurt by Paula's outburst, and the two lived in near silence for a few days. To her credit, Paula realized that she had been unfair in blaming Jane for her own loneliness. Paula apologized to Jane for her unkind words.

Jane wanted to accept Paula's apology—for the sake of harmony in their room, if nothing else. But Jane wondered, *Paula has blown up on me once. What if she keeps on doing that?* For Jane, feeling safe in accepting Paula's apology would require a plan for change. The two talked and finally agreed to the following prevention steps: Paula would either join Jane in making friends or find her own way to make new friends. If either of them felt a frustration beginning to build toward the other, they would talk about the issue before they exploded in anger. Finally, they agreed to plan some fun things to do alone together—just like in the old days.

WHAT IF WE FAIL?

Just because we're working on a plan for constructive change does not mean we will immediately be successful. There are often failures along the road even when we are sincerely trying. These failures need not defeat us.

Rhonda and Jeff have been married for four years. She gives this account of what happened in the early months of their marriage: "We had been married for nine months when Jeff lost his job, which represented 50 percent of our income. He became depressed, as he was unemployed nine and one-half months. During this period, he threatened to leave me. I knew he was depressed, so I tried not to blame him, but it hurt me deeply. He later apologized for threatening to leave me. He told me he knew that was a foolish idea and that he was sorry. He said he would try never to say that again.

"He was successful for about a month. Then one day in the heat of anger, he said, 'I'm not good for you, and I may as well leave.' It created a lot of insecurity in me, and I told him how much it hurt me. The next day, he apologized again and told me that he was just so depressed and down on himself, that it was not my fault. He asked me to pray for him, and he hoped never to talk about leaving again.

"He hasn't brought it up again in over three years. In fact, he has a good job, and we're getting along great. I'm glad I didn't abandon him when he was down. He's a great husband."

Apparently, Rhonda realized that Jeff was trying to save their marriage, so she did not turn on him after he apologized the first time and then failed. However, she did confront him with his failure. He was willing to apologize and try again. One or two setbacks does not mean that you are a failure in following your plan for change. The key is being willing to admit your failures and get up and try again.

'I Can't Believe I Said That'

It's better when you can acknowledge any subsequent failure quickly, even before the offended person has time to confront you. A quick apology indicates that you are sincere in your efforts to change. I met Judy at a marriage seminar in Seattle. She completed one of our apology questionnaires in which she shared this story: "My husband, Steve, criticized me for being afraid of heights. He did it on more than one occasion and in front of other people. It really hurt me. He knew this about me before we got married, but it didn't seem to bother him then. I confronted him about it and told him how much it hurt and embarrassed me, and asked him to please not mention it again. I told him that I was willing to talk to a counselor about it and see if I could get help but, in the meantime, I would appreciate it if he wouldn't mention it. He apologized and agreed that he would never say anything about it again."

Two months later, they were on vacation at the Grand Canyon.

Steve got out on an overlook, very close to the edge, and asked Judy to join him. When she refused, he said, "Look, we flew in an airplane to get out here. Now we are just standing on a rock. It won't hurt you. Come on."

Before Judy could respond, Steve realized what he had said and corrected himself. "I did it again! I can't believe I said that."

His acknowledgment and apology before Judy could even react impressed her as the real thing. "It was so sincere that I truly forgave him." Steve's willingness to admit his failure and apologize again came across loudly and clearly to Judy that he was sincerely trying to change.

On the other hand, when we fail to admit our relapses, it communicates to the spouse that we were not sincere in our apology. Due to shame or embarrassment, we usually don't want to admit our failure, but it is better to acknowledge the relapse up front.

Get Up and Try Again

When in our efforts to change we "fall off the wagon," we must admit our failure as quickly as possible. Get up and try again. This is one of the reasons why Alcoholics Anonymous has been so successful in helping people overcome addiction to alcohol. One of the twelve steps is: "Admit to God, to ourselves, and to another human being the exact nature of our wrongs."[1] Admitting wrong and confessing that wrong to God and another trusted person does require both humility and honesty but gives the opportunity to begin anew.

Some weeks ago, I was playing with my six-year-old granddaughter. She was trying to build a structure from plastic Legos. It kept falling apart at a certain juncture. I could tell she was getting frustrated with the process, so I said to her, "Let me tell you something that my mother told me. 'If at first you don't succeed, try, try again.' Do you understand what that means?" I asked. She nodded and continued to work on the project.

Later that day, I was trying to open a pickle jar and was having difficulty. She looked up at me and said, "If at first you don't succeed, try, try again." I laughed. She laughed and I tried again, this time successfully. It's an important lesson to learn.

Thomas Edison failed many times before he succeeded in inventing the common lightbulb. Babe Ruth struck out far more often than he hit home runs. Lance Armstrong finished last out of 111 riders in his first professional bicycle race.[2] By the time he retired from professional racing in 2005, he had won seven consecutive Tour de France distance races, propelling himself into the record books. The tragedy is that people often give up when they are next door to success. Old behavior patterns die slowly, but we will be successful if we continue to work out our changes.

Anne's Announcement

After ten years of marriage, Anne told her husband one evening she felt he didn't love her. "I don't know how to say this, but I've been feeling for a long time that you don't really love me, that you wish you weren't married to me. It's not a good feeling, and I know it is affecting my behavior toward you, so I guess I'm asking, can we talk about it?"

Bob was shocked, but he welcomed the chance to clear the air. As Anne talked, it became clear she felt that Bob's words of commendation had been replaced by regular criticism . . . and that the words "I love you" had not been heard for a long time.

Bob proceeded to pay her several compliments and then added, "I do love you. I didn't know that you wanted me to keep telling you every day." But they agreed they should visit a counselor.

During their visit in my office, it didn't take long to discover that Anne's love language was words of affirmation and that Bob's vanishing compliments had drained Anne's love tank. Worse yet, he was giving her critical words; at least that's the way she perceived them.

When Bob understood what was going on, he admitted that he had been overly critical the last few months.

"I've been under a lot of pressure at work, and I guess I've taken it out on her. I didn't realize I was coming across so negatively to her, and I certainly didn't realize that she didn't feel loved."

Bob Tries . . .

Bob readily apologized to Anne, and together we worked out a plan for changing Bob's behavior. It seemed that many of his critical comments had come within the first fifteen minutes after he arrived home in the evening. He would see things that hadn't been done and make a comment, or he would express frustration with the behavior of the children. Anne was busy trying to get dinner ready and found these comments quite painful. She proposed the idea of Bob holding his comments on the things he found frustrating until later in the evening when they could sit down in a relaxed manner and talk about them. Bob came up with the idea that he would focus on giving her positive words when he first came home and would try to help with the children while she finished dinner. Anne said, "That would be wonderful."

Two weeks later Bob said to me, "I didn't realize this was going to be so hard. I guess I was more set in my ways than I realized. The first evening when I came home I told Anne how much I appreciated all the work she did around the house and that I was sorry that in the past I was critical and seemed to take her efforts for granted. She smiled, told me she appreciated that, and gave me a kiss. Actually, we had a very good evening.

"However, the second evening I walked in and said, 'Why is Tony playing in the yard by himself? He's only two. He shouldn't be out there alone, and besides that, the neighbor's dog was licking his face.' Anne responded, 'I didn't know he was outside.'

"What do you mean you didn't know he was outside? What have you been doing?" Bob asked her.

"Before I knew what happened, we were into a royal argument and had a miserable evening," Bob said.

...And Tries Again

"The next two evenings, I didn't say anything, positive or negative," Bob continued. "I guess I was discouraged, and it seemed like giving positive words would have been hypocritical. The next day at work, I was thinking about it and realized that if I missed a sale at work, I wouldn't give up on the customer. I would continue to cultivate friendship and seek to make a sale, so why would I give up on seeking to improve things in my marriage? That night I went home and told Anne how much I loved her and that I was sorry that for the last two days I had been silent. I told her that I had been processing things, that I really wanted her to know how much I loved her, and that I was not giving up on changing my behavior. She seemed pleased but not overly excited.

"After that, I began to stop on my way home about a block from my house and ask myself, 'What positive comment will I make to her when I get home?' It may sound a little contrived, but it helped me focus on what I needed to do. So far, I've been pretty successful. I think I had only one relapse this week," he said with a smile.

"And it wasn't very bad," Anne said, also smiling.

A month later, I saw Bob and Anne again and discovered that things were going extremely well. "It's completely different now," said Anne. "I feel loved. I know that he is really trying to change and speak my love language, and he is being really successful. I don't mean he's perfect, but then neither am I, but I do appreciate his change. I really appreciate the way he talks to me now, and we have been able to work through some of the things that have bothered him in the past. I think we're making real progress in our marriage." Bob's efforts at trying again had paid off.

Most people do not expect perfection after an apology, but they do expect to see effort. When the spouse gives up quickly after a failure and reverts to old behavior with no further effort to change, the apology is considered insincere. The person who apologizes may be sincere at the moment, but failure to follow through with repentance renders the apology empty. This is especially true for the person whose primary apology language is repentance.

Thus, expressing your desire to change and coming up with a plan is an extremely important part of an apology to this person. Inviting the offended person to help you come up with a plan for change is perhaps the best way to effectively show repentance. You might say something like the statements on the following page:

Statements of Genuine Repentance

♥ *I know that my behavior was very painful to you. I don't ever want to do that again. I'm open to any ideas you have on how I might change my behavior.*

♥ *How could I say that in a different way that would not come across as critical?*

♥ *I know that what I am doing is not helpful. What would you like to see me change that would make this better for you?*

♥ *I really do want to change. I know I'm not going to be perfect, but I really want to try to change this behavior. Would you be willing to remind me if I revert to my old patterns? Just say "relapse." I think that will help me to stop and change my direction.*

♥ *I let you down by making the same mistake again. What would it take for you to begin to rebuild your trust in me?*

♥ *This is such a long-term pattern for me. While I want to change, I know it will be hard, and I may fail, hurting you again along the way. I would really appreciate it if you would help me think about a way to help my changes stick and encourage me when you see me doing things that help. Can I count on you to be my teammate in this?*

The FIVE LANGUAGES
of APOLOGY

EXPRESSING REGRET
"I am sorry"

ACCEPTING RESPONSIBILITY
"I was wrong"

MAKING RESTITUTION
"What can I do to make it right?"

GENUINELY REPENTING
"I'll try not to do that again"

REQUESTING FORGIVENESS
"Will you please forgive me?"

6

APOLOGY LANGUAGE #5

Requesting FORGIVENESS

Years ago my (Jennifer's) mother worked in a pleasant office setting in Chicago where she got along with all her coworkers. But one afternoon a coworker told her she was bothered by the fact that my mother "never apologizes."

My mother hesitated, then remembered an incident in which she had made a mistake that affected this person. "I felt that I had apologized quickly," Mom told me, "taking responsibility and saying that I was sorry for the inconvenience. So I gingerly asked her what she needed to hear from me."

"Well, you never asked me to forgive you!" the coworker exclaimed.

"Well, I certainly want you to forgive me, because I value our relationship," my mother replied. "So let me ask you now, will you please forgive me?"

She responded, "Certainly." They both laughed, and things once more were fine between them.

My mom recounted the story one sunny March day in the kitchen of my childhood home. She knew Dr. Chapman and I were working on a book, and I had explained the idea of languages of apology. Thinking about her coworker, Mom added: "So I guess she was teaching me how to speak her apology language."

"That's exactly right, Mom. Her apology language was requesting forgiveness. That's what she was waiting to hear from you. I really appreciate your sharing that story. That's what we are finding in our research—that what one person considers an apology is not what another person considers an apology."

When Jennifer told me about this conversation with her mother, I immediately thought of a couple I had counseled several years ago. Angie and Martin had been married nine years when she discovered that he was having an affair with a woman at the office. She confronted him by saying, "I know that you are having an affair with Brenda. I have eyewitnesses, so there is no need to try to deny it." She gave Martin a choice: Either move out of the house within the week or break off the affair and agree to go for counseling. "You can't have both of us. The choice is yours."

Martin left, but within a week, he had come back to say that he wanted to work on the marriage and that he was willing to break off his relationship with Brenda. A few weeks into the counseling process, Angie was saying, "The thing that bothers me is that Martin is not willing to ask me to forgive him. He said that he is sorry, and I really believe that he has broken off the affair with Brenda. I would not be willing to work on the marriage if I didn't believe that. In fact, she has left the company and has told me that she is glad that we are working on our marriage. But Martin will not ask me to forgive him."

"It's like you are trying to make me say those words," replied Martin.

"I'm not trying to make you do anything," Angie said. "But it seems like you are not willing to admit that you are wrong."

"I said it was wrong," replied Martin.

"Then why won't you ask me to forgive you?" she pleaded. "I'm willing to forgive you; I want to forgive you. But how can I forgive you when you don't want to be forgiven? It's as though you don't think you need forgiveness because you haven't really done anything wrong. I don't understand that."

"I know I did wrong," said Martin. "It's just that asking you to forgive me is so hard." He shook his head. Tears came to his eyes and he said, "I don't know why it's so hard!"

It's clear Angie's primary apology language is requesting forgiveness. What she wants to hear is "Will you please forgive me?" To her that is a sincere apology. She is willing to forgive; in fact, she wants to forgive, but she needs assurance that Martin recognizes the need for forgiveness.

But it's also clear that Martin is having a hard time saying those words. Martin is admitting that he finds it difficult to say those words. It is not a language he is accustomed to speaking.

In our research, we discovered that there are lots of Angies in the world. When asked, "What do you expect in an apology?" one of every five (21 percent) answered, "I expect him/her to ask for my forgiveness."[1] For them, these were the magic words that indicated sincerity.

So why is requesting forgiveness so important to some people and such a difficult language for others—like Martin—to speak?

WHY SEEK FORGIVENESS?

Why would requesting forgiveness be so important? Here are the answers that we discovered.

First, requesting forgiveness *indicates to some that you want to see the relationship fully restored.* Ron and Nancy have been married for fifteen years, and Ron indicates that his primary apology language is requesting forgiveness. "When she asks me to forgive her, I know she doesn't want to sweep it under the rug. She wants our relationship to be authentic. Whatever else she says in her apology, I know that when she gets to the place where she asks me to forgive her that she is totally sincere. That's why she makes it easy for me to forgive her. I know that she values our relationship more than anything. That makes me feel really good."

When an offense occurs, immediately it creates an emotional barrier between two people. Until that barrier is removed, the relationship cannot go forward. An apology is an attempt to remove the barrier. If you discover that the person's primary apology language is requesting forgiveness, then this is the surest way of removing the barrier. To that person, this is what indicates that you genuinely want to see the relationship restored.

A second reason that requesting forgiveness is important is that it *shows that you realize you have done something wrong*—that you have offended the other person, intentionally or unintentionally. What you said or did may not have been morally wrong. You may even have done or said it in jest. But it offended the other person. He or she now holds it against you. It is an offense that has created a rift between the two of you. In that sense it is wrong, and requesting forgiveness is in order, especially if this is the person's primary apology language. Asking for forgiveness is an admission of guilt. It shows that you know that you deserve condemnation or punishment.

I met Alma in Tucson. She completed one of our apology questionnaires, and later we talked about it. "How do you know that Bob is sincere when he makes an apology?" I asked. "When he says, 'Will you please forgive me?'" responded Alma. She continued, "Saying 'I'm sorry' does not admit guilt in my eyes. My two-year-old says 'I'm sorry' all the time, but when I ask him to say 'Please forgive me,' his eyes get big and he gulps. Asking for forgiveness admits guilt. Even a two-year-old knows this."

Third, requesting forgiveness *shows that you are willing to put the future of the relationship in the hands of the offended person.* You have admitted your wrong; you have expressed regret; you may have offered to make amends. But now you are saying "Will you forgive me?" You know that you cannot answer that question for that person. It is a choice that he or she must make—to forgive or not to forgive. And the future of the relationship rests on that decision. This takes the control out of your hands, and for some people, this is extremely difficult.

WHAT ARE WE AFRAID OF?

Requesting forgiveness is especially difficult for those individuals who have strong controlling personalities. Remember how Martin had so much difficulty in saying the words "Will you please forgive me" to Angie? When Martin completed a personality test, he and Angie learned he ranked extremely high in the control factor. This means that he felt very uncomfortable when he was not in control of a situation. To ask Angie to forgive him was to relinquish control and put the future of the relationship in her hands. Subconsciously, he found this very difficult.

Eventually Martin realized that the healthy individual is the one who recognizes his/her personality traits, accepts them as being the normal pattern of operation, but refuses to be controlled by these personality traits when they are obviously dysfunctional to a relationship.[2] Therefore, Martin was able to say to Angie, "Will you please forgive me?" She responded with tears, a hug, and a definitive "Yes!" The relationship was restored when he spoke her primary apology language.

Many of us fear rejection, which is another reason it's hard to ask for forgiveness. The fear of rejection is common to humans. Hamilton Beazley, scholar in residence at St. Edward's University in Austin, Texas, and author of *No Regrets*, says, "Apologizing is making an admission that we erred, and we don't like having to do that. . . . It makes us vulnerable because we are requesting something—forgiveness —that we think only the other person can grant, and we might be rejected."[3]

None of us like to be rejected, but for some people, rejection is almost unbearable. For such individuals, requesting forgiveness is extremely difficult because they know that the forgiveness lies in the hand of the other person, and one of the two choices is not to forgive them, which would be rejection.

The answer for this person is to acknowledge this fear—but not to be controlled by it. The reasoning process might go something like this. "I know that my greatest fear is rejection. I also know that my behavior has created a problem in this relationship and that the only way to remove the problem is to sincerely apologize. Therefore, if requesting forgiveness is the apology language of the other person, I will go against my fears and ask, 'Will you please forgive me?'" Mature people recognize their fears but refuse to be held captive by their fears. When they value a relationship, they are willing to go against their fears and take the steps necessary to bring healing to the relationship.

Another fear that sometimes keeps people from requesting forgiveness is the fear of failure. This person typically has a strong moral compass. For them, "doing right" is equated with being good or being successful. Throughout life they have tried to do the right thing. And when they do, they feel successful. To this person, admitting wrong is equivalent to admitting, "I am a failure." Their greatest fear is the fear of failure. To admit in human relationships that they have done wrong seems to be admitting failure. Therefore, they find it difficult to admit they are wrong. Typically they will argue vehemently with the other person that what they did is not wrong. They say, "It may have hurt you," or "It may have offended you." "You took it in the wrong way; I didn't mean it that way."

Sometimes the manner in which they defend themselves is more offensive than the original offense, but they don't see this. They will argue, "I'm just trying to get you to understand the truth." It is this kind of person who almost never apologizes. We were not surprised in our apology research to discover scores of individuals who said, "My spouse almost never apologizes." One husband said, "She's too stubborn to apologize. We've been married ten years, and I've never received an apology from her." A wife said, "I don't know if it's male pride, but he just can't bring himself to apologize unless I give him the silent treatment for a couple of days. He would prefer that both of us be miserable than to admit he is wrong."

The answer for these people lies in coming to understand that fear of failure—like fear of rejection—is one of the most common fears of humankind! The first step is to acknowledge this fear, first to ourselves, saying something like:

"This is one of my fears. This is why I find it difficult to apologize. But I know that no one is perfect, including me. Sometimes I do and say things that offend my spouse or my friend, and it causes a detrimental effect on our relationship. The only way to amend relationships is by apologizing, so I must learn to apologize in spite of my fear. I understand that making a mistake, saying or doing something that offends another person, is something that all of us do. It does not mean that I am a failure.

Fears and Forgiveness

1. Fear of losing control. Some people feel very uncomfortable when they are not in control of a situation. To ask a person to forgive you means to relinquish control and put the future of the relationship in the other person's hands. Subconsciously, you may find this very difficult.

2. Fear of rejection. When you seek forgiveness, the other person may say no— that is, reject your request. That can feel like personal rejection. For some of us, being rejected is our greatest fear.

3. Fear of failure. To admit you are wrong can feel as though you have failed a person, or even failed in keeping your moral beliefs. To those with this fear, admitting wrong is equivalent to saying, "I am a failure."

To admit that what I did was wrong doesn't make me a failure. In fact, it will help me bring healing to my relationship. Therefore, I will go against my fear and apologize. I will admit that I am wrong and I will ask forgiveness."

The person who reasons like this is on the road to becoming a good apologizer and a healthy individual.

As the guest speaker at one of Dr. Chapman's marriage enrichment classes, I (Jennifer) described the five apology languages and indicated that each of us has a primary apology language. At the end of the session, I gave an opportunity for people to ask questions and respond. Lana raised her hand immediately.

"As you began to talk about different apology languages, in my mind I said, 'That's us.' My husband will often say 'I'm sorry' and think he is apologizing. But I will say to him, 'You are not apologizing. You are not saying that you are wrong.'

"As you were talking, I realized we've been speaking different languages. He is saying that he's sorry, and to me that's like it's no big deal. I need for him to ask 'Will you forgive me?' because then it feels like he is admitting his wrong and he is asking me to forgive him. It makes it easier for me to forgive and let the thing go. Before tonight it's like we never had closure whenever one of us hurt the other. We talked about it, and we tried to apologize, but it never seemed to be resolved. Later he would say, 'Well, I said I was sorry. Why are you holding on to this? Why can't you get over it?' I didn't know why I couldn't get over it. It's just that it didn't seem right. Now I get it! I'm so glad we came to this class tonight."

I was very encouraged by Lana's response that night, and I believe this book is going to help thousands of couples learn how to apologize effectively.

REQUEST—DON'T DEMAND!

As difficult as it may be for the offender to ask forgiveness, sometimes it's equally difficult for the offender to realize that the offended may not quickly grant it.

I (Gary) remember the night Jennifer gave her lecture. The response of the class convinced us that we were on the right track. There's a vast difference between requesting forgiveness and demanding forgiveness. In our research, we continually encountered individuals who expected, yes, even demanded that the offended party forget the offense and move on. One wife said, "I can hear it now in my head. I've heard it hundreds of times through our twenty-five years of marriage. He insists, 'I said "I'm sorry." What more do you want?' I just wish that one time he would look me in the eyes and say, 'Will you please forgive me?' He demands my forgiveness, but he never apologizes, and he never changes anything."

I never had an opportunity to talk with her husband, but I had the strong suspicion that he had a controlling personality and a dominant fear of failure. If these two personality traits could have been dealt with, their relationship would not have ended as it did—in divorce.

Don't demand forgiveness. You cannot expect it. When we demand forgiveness, we fail to understand the nature of forgiveness. Forgiveness is essentially a *choice* to lift the penalty and to let the person back into our lives. It is to pardon the offense so that we might redevelop trust. Forgiveness says, "I care about our relationship. Therefore, I choose to accept your apology and no longer demand justice." It is essentially a gift. A gift that is demanded is no longer a gift.

When, as the offender, I demand to be forgiven, I am like a monarch sitting on a throne, judging the offended person as being guilty of an unforgiving heart. The offended person is hurt and angry over my offense, but I am trying to make her feel guilty for not forgiving me. On the other hand, when I go to the offended party and say, "Will you forgive me?" I am now bowing at her throne and requesting to be forgiven of my offense. I know that if she grants my request, I am a recipient of her mercy, love, and grace. Forgiveness is always to be requested but never demanded.

NOT A SMALL THING

Please understand that when you request to be forgiven, you are making a huge request. It will be costly to the person you have offended. When they forgive you, they must give up their desire for justice. They must relinquish their hurt and anger, their feeling of embarrassment or humiliation. They must give up their feelings of rejection and betrayal. Sometimes, they must live with the consequences of your wrong behavior.

These may be physical consequences that need forgiveness, such as a sexually transmitted disease, a child born of a strange lover, or the memory of an abortion. Other consequences may be emotional, such as the mental images of your flushed face and raised voice, the images of you in the arms of another lover, or the cutting words that play over again and again in their minds. The person you have hurt must live with all of this and much more, and process it in order to forgive you. This is not a small thing you're asking of him or her. As an ancient Chinese proverb says, "When you bow, bow low."

Because of the costliness of forgiveness, don't expect the offended person to forgive you immediately. If the offense is minor and if you apologize in the primary apology language of the offended person, then perhaps his or her forgiveness may be extended

---

Why Is It Hard to Forgive?

1. It may require the forgiver to give up a quest for justice. The person may think the offender should "suffer" or does not "deserve" forgiveness. This may be due to physical consequences or feelings of betrayal (see points two and three).

2. The forgiver may need to forgive consequences that are long-lasting. When there are physical consequences, such as abortion or a sexually transmitted disease, or emotional memories, such as a screaming voice or cutting words that replay in someone's mind, the offended will have a difficult time granting forgiveness.

3. The forgiver may have difficulty if the offense is major and/or has been repeated. The granting of forgiveness may require that you follow through with restitution or repentance first, especially if one of these is the offended's primary apology language.

---

rather quickly. But if the offense is major and often repeated, it will take time for the offended party to process your apology, especially if their apology language is the language of restitution or repentance. It takes time to see if you will follow through on making restitution or genuinely repenting and changing destructive behaviors. The person must be convinced of your sincerity, and that may well take time.

In the meantime, your greatest virtue must be patience. Be sure you are (1) speaking the person's primary love language (see chapter 4) and (2) making every effort to change your behavior. If you are consistent in these pursuits, you will likely be the recipient of forgiveness in due time.

Verbally requesting forgiveness *after* you have expressed an apology using some of the other apology languages often is the key that opens the door to the possibility of forgiveness and reconciliation. It may be the one element of your apology that the offended person is waiting to hear. "Will you please forgive me?" is the ingredient that convinces them that you are indeed sincere in your apology. Without the request for forgiveness your statements—"I'm sorry. I was wrong. I will make it up to you. I'll never do it again"—may sound like glib remarks designed to put the matter behind you without really dealing with it. If this is the offended party's primary apology language, then you must learn to speak it if you want her to know that your apology is genuine.

Here are some statements that may help you learn to speak the apology language *requesting forgiveness.*

STATEMENTS REQUESTING FORGIVENESS

♥ *I'm sorry for the way I spoke to you. I know it was loud and harsh. You didn't deserve that. It was very wrong of me, and I want to ask you to forgive me.*

♥ *I know that what I did hurt you very deeply. You have every right never to speak to me again, but I am truly sorry for what I did. And I hope that you can find it in your heart to forgive me.*

♥ *I didn't intend to hurt you but obviously I have. I realize that now, and I see that my actions were wrong even though I was just trying to have fun. It's never right to have fun if someone gets hurt. I promise you I will try to never do that again. And I want to ask you if you will please forgive me.*

In chapter 7, we will give you some questions to ask yourself and others in order to discover your primary apology language. We are also providing a profile (beginning on page 235) to help you discover your primary language of apology. We believe that as family members and friends learn to speak one another's apology language, there will be a whole new level of healing offenses and restoring relationships.

The FIVE LANGUAGES
of APOLOGY

EXPRESSING REGRET
"I am sorry"

ACCEPTING RESPONSIBILITY
"I was wrong"

MAKING RESTITUTION
"What can I do to make it right?"

GENUINELY REPENTING
"I'll try not to do that again"

REQUESTING FORGIVENESS
"Will you please forgive me?"

7

Discovering Your **PRIMARY**
Apology Language

In the last few chapters, we have introduced you to the five languages of an apology—five ways to express your apology. One of these five languages speaks more deeply to us of sincerity than the other four. You may appreciate hearing all five languages, but if you don't hear your primary apology language, you will question the sincerity of the apologizer. On the other hand, if the apology is expressed in your primary language, then you will find it much easier to forgive the offender.

Therefore, it is extremely important to discover your primary apology language and the primary language of the significant people in your life. This will enhance your ability to both give and receive effective apologies.

Understanding the concept of the apology languages has strengthened my (Jennifer's) own marriage. My husband, J.T., is a rational thinker for whom debates are routine and being accurate is of primary importance. Recently, I realized that my apologies should include

"I was wrong" in order for him to best hear my remorse. He needs me to accept responsibility. In contrast, feelings are of central importance to me. I need him to express regret, to say that he is concerned about my feelings: "I am sorry." Now, in our thirteenth year of marriage, we are finally learning to shorten our arguments by apologizing not in our own languages, but in the primary language of the other person.

SPEAKING A DIFFERENT LANGUAGE

What we have learned in our marriage is what Gary and I have found to be true in most marriages: Husbands and wives typically do not have the same primary apology language. Consequently, their apologies are often met with resistance rather than forgiveness.

As I looked at our apology survey data from couples, I reviewed the extent that a husband and wife matched in their primary apology languages. I found that a full 75 percent of the couples *differed* in their most preferred apology language. Amazingly, of that 75 percent who prefer a different language of apology, in 15 percent of the couples one member's primary apology language was the other member's *last choice*! If you apologize to your spouse in the way that *you* most want to be apologized to, our data suggest that, on average, you wouldn't stumble upon his or her favorite apology language until your third attempt! Assuming the survey is accurate, that means three of every four couples must learn to speak an apology language different than the one they most want to hear!

QUESTIONS FOR IDENTIFYING YOUR OWN LANGUAGE OF APOLOGY

First, Jennifer and I want to help you discover your own apology language—the one you would most like to hear when you are offended. Some individuals will know immediately their own primary language of apology. For others, it will not be that easy. Some are like Jim from

Dayton, Ohio, who said, "I don't know my primary apology language because my wife never apologizes. She never thinks she does anything wrong, so why apologize? That was also my father's philosophy. He said, 'Apologizing will get you nowhere. Do the best you can and don't look back.' So, I guess I've never been much of an apologizer either. This is a new concept for me. But I must admit that I wish my wife would apologize for the way she has hurt me. I never thought she would look at another man, let alone get in bed with him. I don't think our marriage can survive unless she sincerely apologizes."

His wife had committed adultery, and Jim naturally—and rightly—rejected his father's philosophy and expected an apology for the breaking of their marriage vows. I (Gary) asked him what he considered a genuine apology.

"I want her to admit that what she has done is wrong and to promise me that she will never do it again. If I knew that she would never do it again, I think I could forgive her."

"I think we've just discovered your primary apology language," I said.

"What's that?" Jim asked.

"Genuine repentance," I replied, adding: "I think if your wife simply said 'I was wrong' but gave you no strong commitment that she was going to change her behavior, you would have a hard time forgiving her. But if she genuinely committed herself not to let it happen again, you could forgive her. More important than anything is that she not continue this extramarital relationship."

"That's it," he said. "I think that's the only way I could really forgive her."

"I think your secondary apology language is accepting responsibility and having her admit that what she did was wrong. It's important to you that she not excuse her behavior."

"I can't accept any excuses," he said. "There is no excuse for what she did."

Question 1: What Do I Expect the Person to Do or Say?

My conversation with Jim illustrates one way to discover your own primary apology language. Ask yourself the question, *What do I expect the person to say or do that would make it possible for me to genuinely forgive them?* You may find that your answer will involve several apology languages.

Janice and Bill were in my office because of an extended argument they had over the fact that he had forgotten their anniversary and had planned nothing special to celebrate it. After listening to both of them for some time, I asked Janice, "What would Bill have to say or do in order for you to forgive him?"

"I want him to say he's sorry," she responded. "I don't think he understands how much this really hurt me. I want him to admit that this was wrong. How could he forget? And it would really be nice if he would try to plan something to make it up to me, something that he would come up with on his own."

"You've mentioned three things," I said. "You want him to tell you that he's sorry. You want him to admit that what he has done is wrong. And you would like for him to do something to make it up to you. If you could only have one of those, which would you choose?"

"More than anything, I want him to know how much this has hurt me," she said. "I don't think he realizes it. Special days are not as important to him as they are to me."

It was obvious to me that Janice's primary apology language was expressing regret. She wanted to hear Bill say, "I realize how deeply I hurt you. I know that our anniversary celebration is important to you. I can't believe I forgot it. I'm really sorry." Then if he would throw in "I hope that you will let me make it up to you," that would be icing on the cake and would definitely start the process of forgiveness in her heart and mind.

Question 2: What Hurts Most Deeply about This Situation?

A second way to discover your primary apology language is to answer the question, *What hurts me most deeply about this situation?* This question is especially helpful if the offender has not yet apologized at all or has not apologized to your satisfaction. Kevin had been hurt deeply by his older brother, Greg. They had always had a close relationship and considered themselves friends as well as brothers. Six months earlier, Greg had gotten a financial tip from one of his buddies at work and had made an investment that had escalated quickly. He shared his good news with Kevin, and to his surprise, Kevin had gotten extremely angry and said, "I can't believe you didn't let me get in on that! I mean, we're brothers. Why didn't you share that with me?"

"I didn't know that you would want to invest," Greg had responded.

"What do you mean, 'don't know if I would want to invest'? Anybody would want to invest in a deal like that!" Kevin said. The conversation went from bad to worse and resulted in the brothers not seeing each other for three weeks. Then Greg went to Kevin and tried to apologize, but Kevin did not respond very positively. They started doing things together again, but the relationship was just not the same. There was a barrier between the two of them. I ran into both of them at a baseball game. They saw me and came over and said, "You are a counselor. Maybe you can help us with a problem we are having." They shared the problem, and I asked Kevin, "What hurts you most about this whole situation?"

"I think it's that Greg will not admit that what he did was wrong. How could you not let your brother in on a good deal? He said he was sorry, but he won't admit that what he did was wrong. That's what hurts me most."

I looked at Greg and he said, "I don't see it as being wrong. In retrospect, I'm really sorry that I didn't let Kevin know, but I wasn't trying to hurt him. I honestly didn't know that he would want to invest.

To be honest with you, I didn't even think about it, and I was surprised when he got upset."

"Do you realize that what you did hurt Kevin very deeply?" I asked.

"I do now," Greg said.

"Is it wrong to hurt one's brother?" I asked.

"Yes, if you do it intentionally," Greg said. "But I didn't do it intentionally."

"I believe that," I said. "Let me ask you a question. If you unintentionally bumped into someone at the office who was holding a cup of coffee and the coffee spilled all over their hand and shirt and floor, what would you say?"

"I'd probably say, 'I'm sorry. I should have been watching where I was walking. Let me help you clean the mess up.' And I'd probably offer to get their shirt cleaned."

"So even though it was unintentional, you would still take the responsibility for your actions by admitting that you should have been watching where you were going, and you would seek to make restitution?"

"Yes," Greg answered, "because obviously I spilled the coffee."

I paused for a moment and then said, "Kevin's coffee is spilled, even though you didn't intend it."

"I've got it," he said. "I should have been watching where I was walking the day I got the tip. If so, I would have shared it with my brother because I really love this guy. And I have not enjoyed the last three weeks."

So as I watched the two in the stands of the big ballpark, Greg looked at his brother and said, "I love you, man. And I should have been thinking about you that day. I'll sell the stock and give you half of the profits."

"Hey, you don't need to do that," Kevin said. "You've already done enough. I forgive you."

The two guys hugged each other, and I was glad that I had come to the ball game.

Had I not asked Kevin the question, "What hurt you most about this situation?" I would never have known that his primary apology language was accepting responsibility. So I would not have known how to have guided Greg in making a sincere apology. Greg did not have to say the words, "I was wrong." He did have to accept responsibility for his actions by saying, "I should have been thinking about you that day." That's what Kevin needed to hear in order to accept Greg's apology as sincere.

I later learned that Greg did sell the stock and gave half of the capital gains to his brother. That was "the icing on the top of the cake." It would not have been necessary, but it sealed the apology and brought further healing to the relationship.

Question 3: What Language Is Most Important When I Apologize?

A third question that will help you discover your primary apology language is, *When I apologize to others, which of the five languages do I think is most important?* This question is based on the assumption that the apology language you speak to others is probably the language you would most wish to receive.

Listen to Mary from Green Bay, Wisconsin: "When I apologize to others, I want to make sure to let them know 'I'm sorry.' I wish it had not happened. I would not want to hurt them in any way, but I realize I have. I want them to know that I'm suffering because I feel very badly that I have hurt them." Mary's own apology language probably is expressing regret.

George is a truck driver from Indianapolis: "When I apologize, I admit that I was wrong. To me, that is what an apology is. If you don't admit that you are wrong, you have not apologized." It's likely George's own apology language is accepting responsibility.

Anna from Charlotte, North Carolina, said, "When I apologize to others, what I try to do is to assure them that with God's help I will not do this again. I want them to know that I am not happy with what I did, and I really want to change my behavior." Anna probably hears an apology best in language #4, genuine repentance that tries to keep the behavior from happening again.

ARE YOU BILINGUAL?

Answering the previous three questions will probably enable you to determine your primary apology language. Perhaps two languages seem to be equally important to you; that is, both speak loudly to you about the sincerity of the other person. When you ask yourself which is more important, you hear yourself say, *Well, really they are equally important*. Then perhaps you are bilingual.

If you are bilingual, that's OK; you will make it easier for those who seek to apologize to you. If the offender speaks *either* of these two languages, you will sense that he or she is sincere and be inclined to forgive the person.

Actually, it is quite common that two or three of the apology languages will be rather important to you. But typically one stands out above the others. If you do not hear your primary language in the apology, you will likely question the sincerity of the apologizer.

To further help you in discovering your primary apology language, we have included an apology language profile on pages 235–46. This is not meant to be a scientific instrument, but it is a practical tool to help you discover your apology language and discuss it with the significant people in your life.

DETECTIVE WORK: DISCOVERING SOMEONE ELSE'S LANGUAGE

How then do you discover the primary apology language of other people with whom you have a relationship? You might encourage them to read this book, answer the three questions given above, or take the apology language profile and discuss it with you. This would be the more overt and probably the most helpful way for the two of you to learn how to apologize to each other effectively.

If, on the other hand, they are not willing to read the book, you could reframe questions 1–3 and use them to discover the person's primary apology language. You could ask the individual to describe an apology that someone once gave him or her that seemed insufficient. In that case, what was lacking? You could ask him, "Was there something the person could have said but chose not to say that would have made your heart feel whole?" Or when you have offended another person, you might ask her: "I know that I have hurt you. I value our relationship. So, what do I need to say or do in order for you to consider forgiving me?" That person's answer will likely reveal her primary apology language.

When her husband asked this question, one wife answered, "I'll tell you one thing. I will never consider forgiving you until you admit what you did was wrong. You act like you can say anything you want to say and it's okay as long as you are joking. Well, I'm tired of your jokes. They hurt me deeply, and I'm never going to forgive you until you acknowledge that they are wrong." Her answer revealed clearly that her primary apology language was accepting responsibility for his behavior and acknowledging to her that what he was saying and the manner in which he was saying it was wrong (language #2).

When you realize that you have offended another person, you might reframe question 2 to sound something like this: "I know that I have hurt you. I can see it in the way you respond to me. I am sorry. It hurts me to know that I have hurt you so deeply. Why don't you tell me what hurts you most about what I said or did?"

The third question is a little more academic and can be asked in a more neutral setting at a time when neither of you have recently offended the other. You might say, "I've been reading a book on apologies and how to give an apology. Let me ask you a question and get your opinion. When you express an apology to someone else for something you've done that has hurt them, what do you think is the most important part of the apology? If you like, I'll give you the five aspects of an apology that are listed in the book."

Three Questions to Help Discover Someone's Apology Language

1. Describe an apology that someone once gave you that you considered insufficient. What was lacking?

2. When you realize you have offended someone, ask: "It hurts me that I have hurt you. Why don't you tell me what hurts you most about what I said or did?"

3. When you express an apology to someone for something you have done that hurt him or her, what do you think is the most important part of an apology?

Here's a bonus question. If you aren't sure after asking the above questions, add this question, with its built-in (and hopefully genuine) compliment: "I value our relationship. What do I need to do or say in order for you to consider forgiving me?"

If they are open, you share the five apology languages. If they say, "I don't want to hear what's in the book. I'll tell you what's important to me," then listen to their answer and you will likely discover their primary apology language.

William, a fifty-three-year-old businessman, was asked this question by a colleague. His response was, "To me, the important part of an apology is letting the other person know that you feel bad that what you have done or failed to do has hurt them." William then recalled a time when he apologized to his daughter for not getting home in time to attend her piano recital.

Seeing her disappointment, he told her, "I realize now how much this meant to you, and I feel really bad that I missed this opportunity to be with you and to watch you perform. I know that you are a great pianist, and I am the loser for not having heard you. I hope that you will forgive me and give me another chance. I love you and your sister and your mom more than anything." He hugged her, and "she cried. I felt that she was trying to forgive me," he told the colleague.

"I felt awful. I tried to communicate that. To me, you are not apologizing if you don't feel awful about what you've done."

This father's answer to his coworker reveals that his primary apology language is expressing regret.

See the sidebar "Three Questions . . ." (plus a bonus question); these questions will help you discover the primary apology language of another person.

A FAMILY PROJECT

Beyond asking these questions, here's a project for family members to help identify one another's apology language. You might start with the father and mother and eventually bring the children into this project (if they are old enough and interested). Spend some time as husband and wife writing down what you think is your own primary apology language. Then list the other four in order of importance. Also, write down what you guess to be the primary apology language of your spouse. You may also list the other four in order of importance, if you wish.

Sit down with your spouse and discuss what you have guessed to be his/her primary apology language. Then tell each other what you consider to be your own primary apology language. Following this, you can look back on times in which you apologized to each other successfully and other times when the apology did not seem to ring true. You can talk about how to apologize to each other in the future. You have now laid the foundation for more effective apologies in your relationship.

Later, you take the children through the same exercise. Have the children list their own primary apology language and the other four in order of importance. Then have them guess the primary language of their siblings and parents.

A GROUP PROJECT

If you are a part of a team at your place of employment or a member of a study group at your church or in your community, we would strongly encourage you to have the group read this book, take the apology language profile at the end (pages 235–46), and discuss this concept with one another. Discovering the primary apology language of the members of the group will greatly increase the effectiveness of your apologies when you have misunderstandings and hurt feelings in the future.

SPEAKING ALL FIVE LANGUAGES

Please don't hear us saying that you should *only* speak the primary apology language of the other person. All of the five apology languages have emotional merit. What we are saying is that you want to be certain that you speak the other person's primary apology language. Then you can sprinkle in the other four languages and get additional emotional credit. But without the primary language, the other languages may not communicate your sincerity. In fact, when you don't know someone's apology language, then you should seek to cover all of your bases. If you genuinely speak each of the five apology languages, you are bound to hit upon something that will be music to the offended person's ears. And they will sense that your apology is sincere.

A '10' APOLOGY

Sincere apologies are a gift to an offended person. They are designed to communicate that you care about your relationship with him or her. They pave the way for genuine forgiveness and reconciliation. Our desire is that this book will help you be more effective in offering sincere apologies when you realize that you have offended someone.

If after you offer your apology, you sense that the other person has not fully forgiven you, here is an approach that may help you deepen the level of forgiveness. A day or two after you have offered your apology, say to the other person, "On a scale of 0–10, how sincere do you feel my apology was the other night?" If the other person says anything less than 10, then you respond, "What could I do to bring it up to a ten?" The answer will give you the practical information you need to continue the apology process until you have done everything possible to pave the way for forgiveness.

One husband asked his wife this question and her answer was, "About seven," to which he responded, "What could I do to bring it up to a ten?" She said, "I mostly believe that you are sincere—but the one thing you didn't say is that you were wrong. I still wonder if you are excusing your behavior because of the way I treated you. I know that I haven't been perfect, but I don't think anything that I have done gave you an excuse to do what you did. I'm not sure that you really feel that."

The husband listened, nodded affirmingly, and said, "I can see how you might feel that way. Let me tell you that I know that what I did was wrong. There was no excuse for my behavior. I take full responsibility for what I did. In no way was it your fault. I'm sorry that I put you through this, and I hope that in time you will be able to forgive me."

And that, very likely, is just what his wife needed to hear.

The FIVE LANGUAGES
of APOLOGY

EXPRESSING REGRET
"I am sorry"

ACCEPTING RESPONSIBILITY
"I was wrong"

MAKING RESTITUTION
"What can I do to make it right?"

GENUINELY REPENTING
"I'll try not to do that again"

REQUESTING FORGIVENESS
"Will you please forgive me?"

APOLOGIZING *Is* *a* **Choice**

But what if . . . ?" Jennifer and I have heard many questions raised when it comes to apologizing. The first is: What if I don't *want* to apologize?

As one man from Bakersfield, California, said, "I know I did wrong, but so did she. In fact, her actions precipitated this whole thing. Why should I apologize when she's the one who started it?"

The problem with the waiting game is that the average life span for men and women is seventy-five years. How much of your adult life do you want to spend in a "cold war" relationship as each of you waits for the other to apologize? I've known couples who have spent thirty years living in the same house but were estranged because each expected the other to make the first move toward an apology.

One husband told me he's spent more than twenty years without his wife or him apologizing to the other. "I don't even remember what the original issue was," he said. "I just know that she insisted that I apologize, and I didn't think I owed her an apology. I thought she was the one who should apologize. Then we argued about who should apologize, and eventually we both fell silent."

Unfortunately, these examples are not uncommon. I know two brothers who haven't spoken to each other in eighteen years because one brother felt the other took advantage of him in a car-trading deal and the other brother said, "I told you the truth about the car." That happened eighteen years ago, and not a word has been exchanged between the two of them since, even though they live in the same town. How tragic when people make a conscious choice not to apologize.

WHY DON'T PEOPLE APOLOGIZE?

'It's Not Worth the Effort'

Why would people choose not to apologize? Sometimes *they do not value the relationship*. Perhaps they have had "run-ins" in the past, and a lot of resentment lies buried underneath the surface. As one lady said about her sister, "I gave up on our relationship. It seemed like no matter what I did, it was never enough and I was always in the wrong. She hurt me on numerous occasions, and I finally decided it wasn't worth the effort. I installed caller ID on my phone so I could identify incoming calls. When she called, I didn't answer the phone. All she ever did was condemn me. It was better not to talk to her. When I go to see my mother, if my sister's car is there, I drive on. I just don't want to get involved."

For a number of perhaps valid reasons, this lady has made the conscious choice to devalue her relationship with her sister. Therefore, she is not motivated to apologize for her own destructive behavior.

'It Was His Fault'

A second reason that people choose not to apologize is that *they feel justified in their behavior; the other person is at fault*. A professional athlete who got involved in a fistfight at a local bar said, "I'm not going to apologize. He shouldn't have made those comments." This athlete's philosophy seems to be, "You do me wrong and you will pay for it. Don't ask me for an apology. You deserved what you got, and don't ever do it again or it will be worse." Obviously, his emphasis was not on building relationships but on exacting revenge. Such an attitude does not remove barriers—it creates them.

This is the infamous tit-for-tat approach to life, and many people practice it. It is in direct contrast to the advice of the Bible to "repay no one evil for evil. . . . If it is possible, as much as depends on you, live peaceably with all men. . . . Do not avenge yourselves . . . for it is written, 'Vengeance is Mine, I will repay,' says the Lord."[1]

The person who justifies her own wrongful behavior is self-deluded. The man or woman who thinks that he/she never does anything that calls for an apology is living in an unrealistic world. The reality is, all of us sometimes make harsh, critical, and unloving statements, and we sometimes behave in hurtful and destructive ways. The person who refuses to recognize the need for an apology will have a life filled with broken relationships.

We came across this attitude over and over again in our research. Here are some examples of what we heard. Betsy from Birmingham said, "Over a ten-year relationship, I have learned not to expect apologies. I have tried to force/coerce them from him, but they are never genuine and he is never repentant. He says that he never does anything to apologize for. So, I have come to accept the fact that I will never get an apology. I just hope it doesn't continue to get worse."

Jamie from suburban Spokane said, "My husband rarely apologizes, because he doesn't see a lot of what he does as wrong. He finds it hard to admit that he makes mistakes."

Martha from Bangor, Maine, said, "My husband is a person of few words. I don't ever remember hearing him apologize. His family never dealt with problems. There are so many hurt emotions in his family and in ours. Things that have been swept under the rug create resentment. As a family, we are just coexisting, because that 'looks' right. I feel like such a hypocrite."

In case you're wondering, this is not just a "guy thing." Women also can refuse to say "I'm sorry." For instance, Jon, who lives in Clovis, New Mexico, said, "Even though I know my wife has done things wrong to me, she always has a way of making me feel guilty. When I think she is about to apologize, the next thing I know she hasn't apologized for anything, but rather has blamed me for her behavior. So I wind up apologizing for her to myself. It's not a very satisfactory apology."

And Mark from Indianapolis said, "My wife never apologizes except when she does something really bad, and even then I don't feel as though she is really sorry."

Often people's consciences have been trained to shift the guilt to someone else. They actually have an *insensitive conscience*, unable to see that the wrong rests with themselves.

Low Self-Esteem . . . and How to Change It

Often an insensitive conscience is *coupled with low self-esteem*. They may have been taught by their parents that apologizing is an indication of weakness. The parents who model this philosophy usually have low self-esteem themselves. They often blame the children for any problems that develop in the family. Consequently, the children develop a sense of low self-esteem and carry this to the next generation. Because they strive so desperately to be a person of worth, and because they associate apologizing as a sign of weakness, they too will blame others for any relationship problems that emerge.

Individuals who suffer from low self-esteem, blame-shifting, and a strong aversion to apologizing will almost always need counseling in order to deal with these deeply ingrained patterns of thought, behavior, and emotions.

What these people do not know is this: Apologizing *enhances* one's self-esteem. People respect the man and the woman who are willing to take responsibility for their own failures. Receiving the respect and admiration of others thus enhances self-esteem. On the other hand, those who try to hide or excuse wrongful behavior will almost always lose the respect and affirmation of others, thus further compounding the problem of low self-esteem. However, the person who is caught up in this negative cycle will find it difficult to understand this reality.

Dave and his wife, Janet, had suffered several significant losses in their lives. When they arrived for their first counseling session with Jennifer, Dave mentioned that he used to be addicted to pornography but was in recovery from that destructive habit. Janet reported feeling very hurt, not only by their recent losses, but also by Dave's long history of secret addiction.

"Has Dave made an adequate apology for the results of his pornography addiction?" I asked. Silence followed, and then Dave explained, "Well, I've said that I'm sorry for my addiction, but I didn't go into any detail, because I just thought that the conversation would go badly." Dave was like a mouse that was caught in a trap; he didn't want to jam himself in further by talking about his misdeeds.

I wanted to help Dave see that, ironically, glossing over the pain that he had caused Janet was only going to prolong everyone's suffering. I explained the concept of "balancing the scales" to Dave and Janet: "When Janet learned of your addiction to pornography, it was as if the scales that kept your marriage in balance flew off-kilter. Her side of the scales plunged to the ground. She felt very low, sad, lonely, angry, and afraid of ever trusting you again. Your general apology was unable to bring your marriage back into balance. Janet continues to feel very hurt and scared. If you leave Janet on the low side of the scales, she is likely to unload the weights that are keeping her down by casting barbs at you."

I concluded my analogy by saying, "Janet needs help in removing the weights from her side of the scale. You could do a great service to her and to your marriage by having the detailed conversation that you fear might go badly. Often, people who will give detailed apologies find just the opposite: As they unload the weights of hurt and validate their spouses, they receive gratitude in return. Janet might loosen her hold on the anger that she has been off-loading onto you. She might find your sincere apology to be wonderfully disarming and helpful."

Dave listened carefully, and it appeared as if a lightbulb had turned on in his mind. He agreed to try a detailed apology at home and to report back the following week.

Dave and Janet arrived the following week with lightness in their steps. Dave had this to say: "I tried what you said, and it wasn't too bad. I explained to Janet how wrong I was to have kept a stash of pornography in the house all these years. I told her that I was sorry that our kids had found my magazines and that it may have damaged them emotionally. I went into other details—my sorrow over having made Janet feel like an inadequate woman, and my betrayal of her trust when I lied about my activities."

Dave was so pleased with his bold move and the freedom it gave him that he told a male friend to do the same: "I've already explained these unbalanced scales to a friend of mine. He needs to apologize to his wife too, and now he says that he will do it!"

Finally, I turned to Janet. "How did it feel to hear these words from Dave?" She replied, "This was an enormous step for Dave. I had given up on ever hearing him take responsibility for his actions. Now, I am more hopeful about the future of our marriage."

Dave added: "For too long, I believed the lie that 'If we talk more about this problem, it will make the situation worse.' I ignored my conscience and, sadly, I sent the message to my wife that I didn't care about her feelings."

Dave was diagnosed with Stage 4 cancer only four months after his apology to his wife. He now marvels, "What if I hadn't apologized to my wife and dealt with this whole issue while I felt healthy? Please tell your readers that there is a real urgency in apologizing while you still have the opportunity to do so!"

Gary and I urge you to seek professional counseling if you fall into these categories: low self-esteem, an underdeveloped conscience, or a tendency to blame others for problems. Your relationships will never reach their potential until you learn to apologize. You are, in fact, deeply hurting the important people in your life because of your unwillingness to apologize.

'WHAT IF I CAN'T LEARN A NEW LANGUAGE?'

A second question we hear often is, "What if the apology language of the other person doesn't come naturally for me?" This is the question that was often raised when we shared the concept of the five languages of an apology. These were very sincere people who wanted to learn to apologize effectively but were being honest to say, "I've never learned to speak that apology language. How difficult is it to learn a language you have seldom spoken?"

It is true that some people will have more difficulty speaking a particular apology language than will others. It all has to do with our history and what we have learned both as children and adults. The good news is all of these apology languages are learnable. We want to introduce you, therefore, to some people who learned to speak an apology language that didn't come naturally for them. Most of them admitted that it was very uncomfortable at first, but they demonstrate the human ability to learn new apology languages.

The Challenge of Expressing Regret

Carl, thinking about marriage, came to one of our seminars with his girlfriend, Melinda. After they completed apology questionnaires, Melinda told him that the thing she wants to hear most in an apology is "I'm sorry."

Later during the seminar, Carl approached me (Gary). "To be honest with you, I don't know if I've ever said those words. They sound kinda girly to me. I've always been taught that real men don't apologize. I guess it is a macho thing.

"I'm not sure I can say those words, and Melinda seems to be concerned about it. Maybe we shouldn't have taken your apology questionnaire!" he joked.

"On the other hand, maybe it's really good that you did," I said with a chuckle. "Let me ask you a question. Have you ever done anything in your whole life that you really regretted? After doing this, did you say to yourself, 'I wish I hadn't done that'?"

He nodded and said, "Yes. I got drunk the night before my mother's funeral. So the next morning, I was suffering with a big hangover. I don't remember much about the funeral."

"How did you feel about that?" I asked.

"Really bad," Carl said. "I really felt like I dishonored my mother. Her death hit me very hard. We had always been close and I could talk with her about things. I guess I was just trying to drown my sorrow, but I had too much to drink. I know that would have made her sad. She always talked to me about drinking too much. I was hoping that people in heaven didn't know what was going on here on earth, because I didn't want to hurt her."

"Suppose for a moment that people in heaven do know what's happening on earth, that your mother really was disappointed in your behavior and what you did. And let's suppose that you had a chance to talk with her. What would you say?"

Carl's eyes moistened, and he said, "I'd tell her that I'm really sorry that I let her down. I know that was not a time for drinking. I wish I could go back and relive that night. I wouldn't have gone to the bar. I'd tell her that I really love her and I hope that she would forgive me."

I put my arm on Carl's shoulder, and I said, "Do you know what you just did?"

He started nodding his head and said, "Yeah. I just apologized to my mother. It feels good. Do you think she heard me?" he asked.

"I think she did," I said, "and I think she's forgiven you."

"Doggone," he said. "I didn't mean to cry," he said, wiping tears from his cheeks.

"That's another thing; you were taught that real men don't cry, right?"

"Yeah."

"You've gotten some bad information through the years, Carl," I said. "Fact is, real men do cry. It's plastic men who don't cry. Real men do apologize. They even say 'I'm sorry' when they realize they've hurt someone they love. You are a real man, Carl. You've demonstrated it today. Don't ever forget it. If you and Melinda get married, you won't be a perfect husband and she won't be a perfect wife. It's not necessary to be perfect in order to have a good marriage. But it is necessary to apologize when you do things that hurt each other. And if saying 'I'm sorry' is Melinda's primary apology language, then you will need to learn to speak it."

"Got it!" he said with a smile. "I'm glad we came to this seminar."

"So am I," I said as he walked away.

One year later, I was leading a seminar in Columbia, South Carolina. Early on Saturday morning before anyone else had arrived, in walked Carl and Melinda. "We came early hoping we would have a chance to talk with you," he said. "We just want to tell you how much your seminar meant to us last year when you were in Summerfield. It was a big changing point in our relationship. We got married three months after the seminar, and the things we learned that day keep coming back to us."

"I'm not sure we would still be married," Melinda said, "if we had not attended the seminar. I had no idea the first year of marriage would be so hard."

"Tell me," I said, "does Carl know how to apologize?"

"Oh, yes. We're both good apologizers," she said. "That's one of the main things we learned that day—that and the five love languages. Those two things have helped us survive."

Carl said, "It wasn't easy for me. But the day I apologized to my mother was a big breakthrough for me. I realized how important it was to be honest about my behavior."

"What is your love language?" I asked Melinda.

"Acts of service," she said, "and Carl is getting really good at it. He even washes and folds the towels."

Carl shook his head and said, "Never thought I'd be doing that. But I'll have to admit, doing laundry is a whole lot easier than saying 'I'm sorry.' But I've learned to do both of them. I want us to have a good marriage. My folks never had a good marriage, nor did Melinda's. Both of us want to grow old together. That's why we're back today for a refresher class. We're looking forward to learning some new things."

"You are a real man," I said as I patted him on the back.

Accepting Responsibility

Marsha admitted it's hard to speak her husband's language, accepting responsibility, especially saying those words, "I was wrong."

"I don't know why," she told me. "Maybe it's because I don't ever remember hearing either of my parents say that, and they didn't teach me how to apologize. They were strong on 'Do your best. Excel. Reach your potential.' But they never said much about apologizing. So I guess I never learned how to speak any of the apology languages."

About a month after she completed the apology questionnaire, she left this message on my Web site: "I've been thinking a lot the last month about the apology languages. Lately it's been on my heart to learn to speak my husband's language, so I've been trying. I have actually said out loud, 'I was wrong. I should not have done that.' But it is still difficult to say, and hard to admit. Each syllable felt like glue in my mouth, but it felt good after I said it, like a weight off my shoulders. It's like I'm beginning to learn how to accept responsibility for my critical words and sometimes hurtful behavior."

Marsha is demonstrating that learning to speak the apology language of the other person is not always easy. She has identified some of the reasons why people find it difficult: It was not modeled by the parents; it was not taught by the parents; in fact, apologizing was not a part of her experience. However, as an adult, she was fully willing to admit that her words and behavior were not always loving and kind. Rather than excusing such behavior, she chose to learn to speak the apology language of her spouse. And it was beginning to make a major difference in the quality of her relationship with her husband.

For those who find it difficult to say the words "I was wrong; I should not have done that," I suggest the following practice. Write the following words on an index card. "I am not perfect. Sometimes I make mistakes. I sometimes say and do things that are painful to others. I know that the other person's primary apology language is hearing me accept responsibility for my behavior by saying, 'I was wrong. I should not have done that.' Therefore, I will learn to say these words."

Read these words aloud. Then repeat the words "I was wrong. I should not have done that" several times alone and aloud in front of the mirror. Breaking the sound barrier and saying something you don't feel comfortable saying is the first step in learning to speak the language of accepting responsibility.

A part of learning to accept responsibility for one's behavior is the realization that no one is perfect. I am imperfect and sometimes do and say hurtful and detrimental things to others. When I choose to admit to myself that I am human and am willing to accept responsibility for the mistakes I make and will apologize using the language of the other person, I am making progress.

Genuinely Repenting

Verbalizing one's intent to repent—"I will work hard to see that this doesn't happen again"—is difficult for some people. Owen was being very honest with me when he said, "I don't want to promise that I'll change, because I might fail. I really do intend to change, or I wouldn't be apologizing in the first place. But when I say that I'm going to try to change, I'm afraid that I'm setting myself up for failure and it will hurt the relationship even more. Why can't I just demonstrate the change rather than talking about it?"

Owen is expressing the sentiment of many. However, the problem of not verbalizing your intention is that the other person cannot read your mind. You know that you are trying to change, but he or she doesn't know. In a very real sense, we verbalize the intention to repent for the same reason that we verbalize the other apology languages. We want the other person to know that we recognize that we have offended her, we value our relationship, and we would like to be forgiven.

Allyson in Mobile, Alabama, expressed it this way: "My husband doesn't see a lot of merit in actually expressing the words 'I'm sorry,' 'I was wrong,' or 'Will you forgive me?' or 'I'll try not to do that again.' But when he does not express the words, I can only assume that he isn't sorry, doesn't realize that he has done wrong, and doesn't intend to change. Even if he is sorry and really is trying to change, I don't know that. Without the words, how do I know that you have really apologized? How do I know that you are really trying to change? For me, repentance is my primary apology language, and if I know that my husband is at least trying to change, I'm willing to forgive him. But if he doesn't tell me, then it's like he is not speaking my apology language, and I have a hard time believing that he is sincere."

Allyson is making it clear that expressing the intention to try to change is the first step in speaking the apology language of repentance.

I am not suggesting that you promise that you will never do it again. What you are expressing is that you are going to make every effort not to repeat this behavior. It is effort that leads to success. Changing long-standing patterns of behavior can be difficult. But the first step is deciding that they need to be changed and, with the help of God, you will start walking down the road toward positive change. Most people will be encouraged by your efforts and will be willing to forgive you when you stumble along the road if you are willing to confess the failure.

Don't allow the fear of failure to keep you from taking the first steps down the road of repentance and success. If this is the other person's primary apology language, nothing will take the place of the words "I'm really going to try hard to change this behavior." Then developing a plan and following that plan leads you further down the road to success and the healing of past hurts.

'WHAT IF I AM OVERLY APOLOGETIC?'

The third question I want to address is: What if you tend to be overly apologetic? In our research, we continued to encounter individuals who admitted that they or their friends tended to apologize almost daily. Any time there was any sense of tension between them and another person, they immediately apologized.

'I Shoot Myself in the Foot'

People who tend to be overly apologetic do so for differing reasons. Some individuals apologize frequently because they are frequently guilty of words or actions that inflict pain on others. Jordan told me, "I have more experience apologizing than my wife does because I am constantly shooting myself in the foot. I'm a rather talkative person. And sometimes that gets me in trouble. I say things without thinking and later realize that I have hurt my wife or someone at work. So I do a lot of apologizing."

Emma says her husband, Andrew, apologizes regularly for a similar reason: "He does something to apologize for every day."

I thought at first she might be joking, but I didn't see a smile on her face. So I said, "You are serious, aren't you?"

She said, "Yes. I never met a man who was so insensitive. But he's quick to apologize. I just wish he could learn to stop doing things he has to apologize for."

For people like Jordan and Andrew, the problem does not lie in an unwillingness to apologize but rather in a deficiency in relationship skills. They have learned to cope with this deficiency by frequently and freely apologizing. A more satisfying and long-term answer would be for these individuals to attend classes on how to build better relationship skills, go for individual counseling, and/or read books on the fundamentals of relating positively to other people.

'I Assume It's My Fault'

Others who tend to overly apologize are suffering from low self-esteem. Lucy is a thirty-five-year-old single who said, "I usually feel as if everything is my fault—at work, at home, and in all of my relationships. I guess I never felt very good about myself. So when things go wrong in relationships, I just assume it is my fault. So I apologize. People often say to me, 'You don't need to apologize for that. You didn't do anything wrong.' But I always feel like I am in error."

Patricia lives in Phoenix. She and her husband retired early and moved from Michigan to a warmer climate. She said about her husband, "Dave constantly apologizes by saying 'I'm sorry.' But it is with the attitude 'I know I'm worthless and I can't do anything right.' Obviously, he is not worthless. He is a great businessman; otherwise, we would not have been able to retire early. And he doesn't do a lot of things that call for an apology. I think it is probably just low self-esteem on his part. But it takes away from the apology. And often, it makes the situation worse because I don't feel it is a heartfelt 'Please forgive me. I didn't mean to hurt you.' Instead it is an 'I'm sorry; I'm an idiot; what can I say?'"

I never had an opportunity to talk with her husband, Dave, but I had the sense that he was either suffering from low self-esteem derived from his childhood experience or that his excessive apologies were his way of responding to an overly critical wife who had found fault with him through the years, and his way of coping was simply by accepting the condemnation. In either scenario, he was suffering from a self-esteem problem. The road to a better relationship would likely lead through a counselor's office where Dave could deal with his self-perceptions and come to a new and more positive under-standing of who he is. He was locked into a pattern of low self-esteem that did not need to continue for the rest of his life.

'I Want to Get It Over With'

A third category of overly apologetic people are those who strongly dislike conflict and want to get the issue settled quickly so that things can "get back to normal." They are willing to accept responsibility and apologize even if they do not sense that they are at fault simply to get the issue settled. They don't like the emotional discomfort that comes from long discussions about the issue. They would much rather apol-ogize, accept the responsibility, and hope that they can move on. Here are some examples from our research of people who fall into this category.

"If I want to sleep, then I have to get it over with," says Mildred, married to Bruce for twenty years. "I find that I apologize [to Bruce] even when I am the one who is not in the wrong, just so I can end the fight and wake up with a clean conscience."

Calvin is from New York City and was attending a marriage enrichment event that I was leading. He said, "My parents were non-confrontational when I was growing up. I'm not used to seeing dis-putes. So when I get upset or disappointed, I feel I have to apologize and set things right. I grew up Catholic, and I loved the sacrament of confession. I just felt good about confessing aloud and being forgiven."

Jonathan is twenty-five, has been married for two years, and really enjoys his job. "I don't always have to win, and I don't like confrontation. I will apologize even if it is not my fault because I want to move on. I don't want to waste time arguing. I guess I'm a lover, not a fighter."

Interestingly, several people told me the "best apologizer" was the one who apologized the most—even if the apologizer was not at fault. When I asked Suzanne, "Who is the best apologizer, you or your husband?" she said, "My husband is by far the best apologizer in our marriage. In fact, I would say that he apologizes 90 percent of the time, even when it is not his fault. He wants peace between us, so he is usually the one to make up first."

Similarly, Adrianne told me, "My husband is the best apologizer, because he does not want there to be any friction between us. He can't stand arguments."

Don said his wife, Denise, is the best apologizer. "She doesn't like to continue an argument/disagreement beyond the initial confrontation. She doesn't feel it's over until someone apologizes, so she will do so, even if she feels it's my fault."

Don found those apologies annoying. "She drives me crazy. I want her to fight with me, but she chooses to apologize."

Denise explained, "I just want to make the tension go away."

A 'Peace' That Leads to Resentment

For these and thousands of others like them, they desire peace at any price. They would rather admit wrong if the arguments and conflicts will cease. Emotional calmness is more important than being right. While this may appear to be an admirable trait, it often simmers as inner resentment.

Jan and Kent have been married for fifteen years and live just outside Williamsburg, Virginia. She said, "I am the one who seems to apologize most in our marriage. Kent is not good at verbalizing his feelings. And in order to get past whatever it is that went wrong and caused hard feelings, I usually end up apologizing just so we can get back on speaking terms again. I often end up internalizing hard feelings because I have to apologize, even when I'm not the one who caused the problem."

Such internalized resentment often creates emotional distance between two individuals. On the surface things seem to be relatively calm, but underneath an emotional explosion is in the making.

If an individual senses such emotional resentment building, it is time to talk to a counselor, pastor, or trusted friend. Failure to process the resentment can lead to the destruction of a relationship. Peace at any price is not the road to authentic relationships. Apologies need to be sincere. When we apologize simply to avoid facing an issue rather than seeking genuine reconciliation, the apology ceases to be sincere. Remember, the purpose of apologies is to receive forgiveness and reconciliation with the person you have offended.

In chapter 9 we will look at the other side of the coin—forgiving those who apologize. We will also address the question, "What if the other person does not apologize for his or her wrong or hurtful behavior?"

The FIVE LANGUAGES
of APOLOGY

EXPRESSING REGRET
"I am sorry"

ACCEPTING RESPONSIBILITY
"I was wrong"

MAKING RESTITUTION
"What can I do to make it right?"

GENUINELY REPENTING
"I'll try not to do that again"

REQUESTING FORGIVENESS
"Will you please forgive me?"

9

Learning to FORGIVE

In this chapter, we move from *making* an apology to *accepting* the apology. As we've seen, forgiving someone for wrong behavior can be tough, especially if we consider the offense to be major.

Let's be clear: The need for forgiveness always begins with an offense. The International Forgiveness Institute, founded by Professor Robert Enright, a pioneer in "forgiveness" research, defines forgiveness as a moral issue: Forgiveness "is a response to an injustice (a moral wrong)," and "it is a turning to the 'good' in the face of wrongdoing."[1] If no offense has been committed, then forgiveness is a non-issue.

All sincere apologies have the same two goals: that the offender be forgiven and the relationship be reconciled. When forgiveness and reconciliation occur, the relationship can continue to grow.

Granting forgiveness is much easier if the person who offends you speaks your primary apology language. However, forgiveness is still a choice. When you and I receive an apology, we can choose to forgive or not to forgive.

LIKE A BOMB FALLING

Even a minor offense can be like a bomb falling on a picnic. It destroys the tranquility of the relationship. If you're the one offended, you know how it feels: There's hurt, anger, disappointment, disbelief, a sense of betrayal and rejection. Whether the offender is a coworker, roommate, parent, or spouse, the question is, *How could they love me and say or do that?* Your love tank has just suffered a rupture.

There's more fallout: Your sense of justice has been violated. It's like little moral soldiers inside you stand up and say, "That's not right. We will fight for you." Everything in you wants to say to those little soldiers, "Charge!" But you are not sure that is the right thing to do. You value this relationship. You think, *Maybe they didn't mean it like it sounded,* or *Maybe I didn't get the full story.*

Reason prevails as you try to gain information. Perhaps you find that you were mistaken. You read the situation incorrectly. So, your anger subsides and you continue to develop the relationship. On the other hand, investigation may confirm your worst fears. It is real, and it is worse than you thought. The person has wronged you. He has hurt you; she has humiliated you. Her words were unkind, unloving, and disrespectful. The offense now sits as an emotional barrier between the two of you.

Often the situation is compounded by our response. She screamed at you, so you scream at her. She pushed you, so you push her. She said something disrespectful to you, so you reciprocate. Now you are both guilty of an offense. Unless each of you chooses to apologize and each of you chooses to forgive, the emotional barrier will never be completely removed.

Because we are all imperfect, we sometimes fail to treat each other with love, dignity, and respect; apologies and forgiveness therefore are essential elements to healthy relationships. Who apologizes first is unimportant. *That* each of you apologizes is all-important. An apology reaches out for forgiveness. So let's look at the art of forgiving.

WHAT IS FORGIVENESS?

First, let's clarify the meaning of the word *forgiveness*. Three Hebrew words and four Greek words are translated *forgive* in the English Scriptures. They are basic synonyms with slightly varying shades of meaning. The key ideas are "to cover; to take away; to pardon; and to be gracious to."

The most common of these is the idea of taking away one's sins (failures). For example, the psalmist says, "As far as the east is from the west, so far has he removed our transgressions from us."[2] This psalmist is speaking of God's forgiveness; thus, God's forgiveness is relieving the person from God's judgment—from the penalty due the person who transgresses God's law. Again the Scriptures say, "He does not treat us as our sins deserve or repay us according to our iniquities."[3] Isaiah the prophet spoke of God "blotting out" our sins and remembering them no more.[4] Clearly, God's forgiveness means that our sins no longer stand as a barrier between us and God. Forgiveness removes the distance and allows us open fellowship with God.

The same is true in human forgiveness. Forgiveness means we choose to lift the penalty, to pardon the offender. It means letting go of the offense and welcoming the offender back into your life. Forgiveness is not a feeling but a decision. It is the decision to continue growing in the relationship by removing the barrier.

If you're the offended party, forgiveness means that you will not seek revenge, that you will not demand justice, that you will not let the offense stand between the two of you. Forgiveness results in reconciliation. This does not mean that trust is immediately restored. We will talk about that later. Reconciliation means that the two of you have put the issue behind you and are now facing the future together.

THE FORGIVENESS CYCLE

An apology is an important part of *the forgiveness cycle*. An offense is committed; an apology is made; and forgiveness is given.

A Divine Model

Again, this cycle is clearly seen in God's relationship with people. The prophet Isaiah delivered this message to ancient Israel. "Your iniquities have separated you from your God; your sins have hidden his face from you, so that he will not hear."[5] We are never separated from God's love, but our disobedience does separate us from His fellowship. The New Testament reminds us that "the wages of sin is death."[6] Death is the ultimate picture of separation. Of course, this is not what God desires for His creatures. Therefore, the writer quickly adds that "the gift of God is eternal life in Christ Jesus our Lord."[7] God desires fellowship with His creatures; that is what the cross of Christ is all about. God offers His forgiveness freely.

In order to experience God's forgiveness, people must respond by *repentance* (a turning around) and faith in Christ.[8] The message is clear. If we would receive God's forgiveness, we must acknowledge our sin and accept His forgiveness. John the apostle writes, "If we confess our sins, [God] is faithful and just and will forgive us our sins."[9] Thus, in order for our fellowship with God to be restored, we must acknowledge our sin—that is, apologize. The moment we do this, we experience the warm embrace of our heavenly Father. The distance is gone. We are again walking in fellowship with God.

I have taken time to review God's forgiveness toward us because the Scriptures say that we as humans are to forgive each other as God forgives us.[10] That's the divine model, and it is a wise and prudent model for making an apology in today's world. It has two essential elements: (1) confession and repentance on the part of the offender, and (2) forgiveness on the part of the one sinned against.

In the Scriptures, these two are never separated. Therefore, on the human level, the apology is a critical element in the cycle of forgiveness. That is why we have spent the first half of this book talking about how to apologize effectively. However, once the apology is made, the offended person then has a choice: to forgive or not to forgive. To forgive opens the door to reconciliation between the two of you. Not to forgive leads to further deterioration of the relationship.

Jesus declared to His followers, "Do to others what you would have them do to you, for this sums up the Law and the Prophets."[11] Most of us would like to have forgiveness when we fail. Therefore, we are encouraged to extend forgiveness to those who offend us. The Christian message is that we can forgive because we have been forgiven by God. God forgives us because Christ paid the ultimate penalty for our failures. Therefore, our capacity to forgive others comes from God. It is always proper to pray, "Lord, help me to forgive."

The Ideal: Take the Initiative to Apologize

The ideal scenario is that when we have offended others, we take the initiative to apologize.[12] In our relationship with God, the Scriptures encourage us to judge our own sin before God moves to judge us.[13] Likewise in human relationships, we should be quick to confess our failures and seek forgiveness.

When No Apology Is Offered

What if the person who offended me does not come back to apologize? Then I am to lovingly confront the offender. This approach was laid out clearly by Jesus. "If your brother sins against you, rebuke him; and if he repents, forgive him. And if he sins against you seven times in a day, and seven times in a day returns to you, saying, 'I repent,' you shall forgive him."[14] The pattern is clear. An offense is committed. The person does not immediately apologize. So you confront the offender, looking for an apology. If the person apologizes, then you forgive. There is to be no limit to our forgiveness so long as the offender returns to apologize.

What if the offender refuses to apologize—even when confronted with his/her wrong behavior? We are to approach the person a second time, telling them of the offense and giving them opportunity to apologize. Again, Jesus gave clear instructions to His followers. "If your brother sins against you, go and tell him his fault between you and him alone. If he hears you, you have gained your brother. But if he will not hear, take with you one or two more . . ."[15]

Again, the pattern is clear. You approach the person a second or even a third time. Each time you are willing to forgive and seeking reconciliation. Ultimately, the offender may be unwilling to acknowledge the need of forgiveness and refuse to apologize for the wrong behavior. Even then, the Christian is to pray for them, seek to communicate the love of Christ, and hope that they will repent of their wrongdoing and experience forgiveness.

Please notice carefully that Jesus did not say we should forgive the offender when he or she is unwilling to apologize. Notice also that Jesus was addressing the issue of moral sin—"If your brother sins against you." Some of our irritations in relationships are simply that— irritations. Our spouse doesn't load the dishwasher the way we do. We may request change, but if our spouse does not, it is not a moral failure. Many of the irritations in relationships we can overlook, forbear, accept. But moral failures always stand as a barrier that can be removed only by apologizing and forgiveness.

Therefore, if a person refuses to apologize for a moral failure after being confronted several times, we are to release the person who has sinned against us to God, letting God take care of the person rather than insisting that we pay back the individual for the wrongful action. The Scriptures teach that vengeance belongs to God, not to man.[16] The reason for this is that God alone knows everything about the other person, not only his actions but his motives—and God alone is the ultimate judge.

Releasing the Person to God

So the person who is feeling hurt and angry toward another who has treated him unfairly is to release that person to an all-knowing heavenly

Father who is fully capable of doing what is just and right toward that person.

Jesus Himself gave us the model. The apostle Peter said of Jesus, "When they hurled their insults at him, he did not retaliate; when he suffered, he made no threats. Instead, he entrusted himself to him who judges justly."[17] Or as Weymouth translates it, "He left His wrongs in the hands of the righteous Judge."[18] As a man, Jesus did not take revenge on those who had wronged Him; rather, He committed the whole situation to God, knowing that God would judge righteously.

Often when we have been wronged, we think that if we don't press the issue and demand justice, then no one will. You can turn your erring friend and the wrong committed against you over to God, knowing that He will take the best possible action on your behalf. He is more concerned about righteousness than you are.

Once you have released the person to God, then it is time to confess your own sin. Remember, hurt and anger are not sinful. But often we allow anger to lead us to sinful behavior. Explosive words or destructive behavior must be acknowledged to God and to the person you sinned against. Don't allow the other person's refusal to apologize to keep you from apologizing. He or she may or may not forgive you, but when you have apologized, you will be able to look yourself in the mirror knowing that you are willing to admit your failures.

FORGIVING WHEN THE APOLOGIZER DOESN'T SPEAK YOUR LANGUAGE

What if the person apologizes but she doesn't speak your primary apology language? This is often the case. In fact, this is what motivated us to write this book. We believe that there are thousands of people who offer sincere apologies, but they are not understood to be sincere because they fail to speak the other person's primary apology language.

It would be ideal if everyone could read this book and learn to speak one another's primary apology language. However, until that happens, perhaps your understanding of the five languages of an apology will help you see their heart. Perhaps they are sincere and are apologizing in the only language they know. This insight may help you forgive them even when they don't speak your language.

I remember the mother who said, "After I heard you speak about the five languages of an apology, it was much easier for me to forgive my adult son. He is thirty years old, and he has apologized many times. But all he ever says is 'I'm sorry.' To him, that is an apology. To me, that leaves a lot to be desired. I want to hear him say, 'I was wrong; will you please forgive me?' But he always stops with 'I'm sorry.'

"In the past, I've forgiven him most of the time. But I always had questions about his sincerity. After your lecture, I realized that he was sincere, that he was speaking his apology language. And even though it was not mine, I believe he was sincere. So it made it easier for me to genuinely forgive him."

THE DANGER OF FORGIVING TOO EASILY

Some of us have been trained since childhood to forgive quickly and freely. If a person makes an apology using any of the apology languages, we are likely to forgive him and not question his sincerity. In so doing, we may end up encouraging destructive behavior.

Lisa and her husband, Ben, faced what she called "many stressors" in their first year of marriage: moving to a new city, selling one house and buying another—twice. Lisa had ongoing health problems; Ben had a new job, his parents separated, and his father threatened to commit suicide; and together the two started a singles' ministry in their church. In Lisa's letter to me (Jennifer), she described the final major setback: "Last, my husband committed adultery."

I read Lisa's letter closely: "I felt God instructed me to forgive him and love him. I did. I reasoned that after all that we had been through, anyone could make a mistake. I freely gave my forgiveness and spoke of this affair only two more times. However, a year later he cheated with another woman. This time I gave him a hard time, and some consequences were handed out. My pastor got involved. We both showed him love and mercy, and I forgave him after he said he was sorry and 'repented.'

"Eight years went by and, unknown to me, my husband continued his affairs. An awakening phone call came from him, saying, 'I am in love with another woman, and I'm not coming home tonight.' At that point, I changed all the locks and had him in the lawyer's office signing separation papers."

Lisa and Ben had a year's separation. During that time, they began to repair their wounded marriage. "By a miracle of God, much counseling, and setting more healthy boundaries, we are affair free—and celebrating fourteen years of marriage," she said.

Yes, that is an amazing ending, and Lisa would say God was in the saving of their shaky marriage. Still, she has regrets that Ben's deception continued as long as it did and that she had not taken stronger action sooner. "I believe if I had known about the five languages of apology and had been a better judge of sincerity, my boundaries would have been stronger earlier in the marriage. I would have been less codependent and weak in the name of forgiveness. My discernment of true repentance would have been enhanced, and it might have saved us many years of unbearable sorrow."

I think Lisa is right. Holding someone accountable for negative behavior is an act of love. Had Lisa understood the five languages of apology, she likely would have had the courage to say after the first offense, "I love you too much to take this lightly. I will not continue in this relationship unless we can agree to get extensive counseling. Our relationship is too important to me to treat this as a light offense." In major moral failures, we must deal with the cause of the behavior if we expect there to be genuine, long-term change.

'I NEED SOME TIME'

Earlier we indicated that there are two common responses to an apology: to forgive or not to forgive. In reality, there is a third possible response: "Give me some time to think about it. I want to forgive you, but I've got to have some time to process all of this."

Sometimes we have been hurt so deeply or so often that we cannot bring ourselves emotionally, spiritually, or physically to the point of genuinely extending forgiveness. We need time for inner healing, for the restoration of emotional balance, or sometimes physical health that will give us the capacity to forgive. I (Gary) remember the husband who said, "After my wife's first lie about her drug use, I chose to forgive her and to work on our marriage because I thought she truly regretted what she had done. I was convinced that she would never do it again. But now, she has done it again and again. She entered a treatment program but left three weeks before the program was over. She said she could make it on her own. Well, she didn't. Within a week, she was stoned again.

"This time she is asking me for another chance. She says she will stick with the program. I've agreed to pay for the treatment, but I don't know if I can forgive her. I'm overwhelmed. I'm willing to pray about it, but right now I don't want to see her."

I felt great empathy for this husband. Who would not understand his reluctance to forgive? Who would be so calloused as to demand that he forgive her on the spot? Who can give him the assurance that her apology is sincere? And who can assure him that it will never happen again? All the evidence seems to point in the opposite direction.

"I love my wife," he said, "and she says that she loves me. But how can that be? How can you do this if you love someone? It's a strange way to show love. I hope in time that I can forgive her. I hope that she is sincere. I hope that she has realized that she has been walking the wrong road. But right now, I don't know."

This is a husband who deep within wants to forgive his wife. He wants to have a genuinely loving relationship, but he doesn't know if he can forgive her. Time will tell. He is open to the possibility, and he is praying and waiting. Sometimes, this is the only realistic approach to forgiveness. In the meantime, he must process his emotions with God and not allow his hurt to turn into bitterness and hatred.

TRUST: THE TENDER PLANT

This brings us to the issue of rebuilding trust. Forgiveness and trust are not to be equated. Because forgiveness is a decision, it can be extended immediately when one perceives he has heard a sincere apology. However, trust is not a *decision*—it is rather an *emotion*. Trust is that gut-level confidence that you will do what you say you will do.

Obviously, trust has a cognitive aspect: "I choose to believe that you are a person of integrity" is a statement based on trust. However, this statement is rooted in the soil of emotions. Trust is that emotional sense that I can relax with you and don't have to be suspicious. I can let down my emotional guard because you will not knowingly hurt me.

In most relationships, trust develops in the early stages of the relationship. Unless we have been deeply hurt in the past, we tend to assume that people are who they claim to be. If in the early months of the relationship we find no occasion to doubt that, then our initial trust is affirmed and deepened.

Trust, then, is one's normal emotional state in healthy relationships. Friends trust each other. Spouses trust each other. Close vocational associates usually trust each other. However, when trust is violated or betrayed, it does not spring back immediately after an apology and the extending of forgiveness. Trust is diminished because the person proved to be untrustworthy. If I am honest, I will likely say, "I forgive you because I believe you are sincere in your apology. But to be very honest, I don't trust you as deeply as I did before."

I like to visualize trust as a tender plant. When trust is violated, it is as though someone stepped on the plant and pushed it into the mud. The rain and the sun may eventually enable the plant to stand erect again, but it will not happen overnight. So how do we rebuild trust in a relationship when it has been violated? The answer is by being trustworthy one day at a time. A sincere apology and genuine forgiveness open the door to the possibility of trust growing again. How does this happen? In my experience in working with couples through the years, it is fostered best when the offender chooses to open his/her private life to the scrutiny of the offended spouse.

For example, if the offense was in the area of money, then the attitude will be "Here is the checkbook; here is the savings account; here are the stockholdings. You may look at these anytime you wish. I have no other accounts. I will introduce you to the people who manage these accounts and let them know that you have total access."

If the offense was in the area of sexual unfaithfulness, then you allow the partner full access to your cell phone, computer, and any other means of communication. You give a full accounting of all of your time. And you give your spouse permission to make phone calls to affirm that you are where you said you would be. Trust is not fostered by secretiveness but by openness. If you choose to be trustworthy over a period of time, your spouse will likely come to trust you again. If you continue to be untrustworthy by lying, cheating, hiding, and making excuses, trust will never be reborn. Trust's only hope of survival is the rain and sunshine of integrity.

Because the rebuilding of trust is a process and takes time, people have sometimes said to me, "I think I've forgiven my spouse. But some days I feel like I haven't, because I really don't trust them." Their struggle comes because they are confusing forgiveness and trust. In summary, forgiveness is a choice to lift the penalty and allow the person back into your life so that the relationship can continue to grow. Trust, on the other hand, returns in stages. When there is changed behavior over a period of time, you begin to feel more comfortable and optimistic about the other person. If this continues, eventually you will come to trust them fully again.

COMPLETING THE CYCLE

Forgiveness holds the power to give renewed life to the relationship. The choice not to forgive pronounces the death penalty upon the relationship. Without forgiveness, relationships die. With forgiveness, relationships have the potential for becoming vibrant and enriching the lives of the people involved.

It would be hard to overestimate the power of forgiveness. It is the goal of every sincere apology. If forgiveness is not extended, then the apology hangs as a loose electrical wire disconnected from the system. An apology alone cannot restore relationships. An apology is a request for forgiveness. It is the gift of forgiveness that ultimately restores the relationship. If we are friends and you violate our friendship by treating me unfairly but quickly come to me with a sincere apology, the future of our relationship is neither determined by your offense nor by your apology but by my willingness or unwillingness to forgive you. Forgiveness completes the cycle and leads to reconciliation. Without forgiveness, the purpose of the apology is thwarted.

WHAT FORGIVENESS CAN'T DO

Let me be quick to add that forgiveness does not remove all the results of failure. If a man is given to fits of anger and strikes out at his wife, hitting her on the chin and breaking her jaw, he may sincerely confess and she may genuinely forgive. But her jaw is still broken and may cause her difficulty for years to come. If a teenage girl, in spite of her parents' urging, succumbs to trying a popular drug at the request of a friend and that drug adversely affects her mental capacity, the friend, who offered the drug may apologize sincerely and profusely. The girl may apologize to her parents if she has the mental capacity to do so. The parents may genuinely forgive, but the mental capacity of the young girl is forever impaired.

It is one of the fundamental realities of life: When we commit actions or speak words that are detrimental to another, the consequences of those actions and words are never fully removed, even with genuine forgiveness.

The second reality is that forgiveness does not remove all painful emotions. A wife may well forgive her husband for striking her in anger. But when she thinks about what he did, she may once again feel disappointment, hurt, and rejection. Forgiveness is not a feeling; it is a commitment to accept the person in spite of what he or she has done. It is a decision not to demand justice but to show mercy.

Forgiveness does not remove the memory of the event. We speak of forgiving and forgetting. But ultimately, we never forget. Every event in life is recorded in the brain. There is every potential that the event will return to the conscious mind again and again. If we have chosen to forgive, we take the memory to God along with the hurt feelings, acknowledge to Him what we are thinking and feeling, but thank Him that by His grace the offense has been forgiven. Then we ask God for the power to do something kind and loving for that person today. We choose to focus on the future and not allow our minds to be obsessed with past failures that are now forgiven.

Assuming you are ready to express forgiveness, how might you verbalize it? On the next page are some suggestions.

STATEMENTS OF FORGIVENESS

♥ *I am deeply hurt by what you said. I think you realize that. I appreciate your apology, because without it, I don't think I could forgive you. But because I think you are sincere, I want you to know that I forgive you.*

♥ *What can I say? I'm touched by your apology. I value our relationship greatly. Therefore, I'm choosing to forgive you.*

♥ *I didn't know if I would ever be able to say this sincerely. I was devastated by what you did. I would never have imagined you capable of doing such a thing. But I love you, and I choose to believe that your apology is sincere. So I am offering you my forgiveness.*

♥ *Your work error has cost me both time and money. I want to forgive you for causing this problem. Yes, I believe that with your correction plan in place, I can forgive you.*

♥ *I know how hard it is for you to swallow your pride and say, "I was wrong." You've grown in my eyes, and I do forgive you.*

The FIVE LANGUAGES
of APOLOGY

EXPRESSING REGRET
"I am sorry"

ACCEPTING RESPONSIBILITY
"I was wrong"

MAKING RESTITUTION
"What can I do to make it right?"

GENUINELY REPENTING
"I'll try not to do that again"

REQUESTING FORGIVENESS
"Will you please forgive me?"

10

Learning to APOLOGIZE
in the Family

Without a sincere apology, broken relationships stay broken. And there are many broken relationships within families. Young adults are often estranged from their parents. Brothers have not talked to each other in fifteen years. Parents verbally or physically abuse their children and then are unwilling to apologize, allowing the children to grow up with a sense of parental rejection. I (Gary) encounter numerous husbands and wives who treat each other harshly, refuse to apologize, and eventually live lives of quiet desperation.

We believe that the insights contained in this book could help many of these family members reconnect emotionally. In fact, the real-life examples of individuals who have chosen to apologize prove family relationships can be renewed and restored.

Of course, even sincere apologies do not always result in forgiveness and restoration; yet without an apology the relationship almost certainly will remain fractured.

When you are willing to apologize for your part in the offense, you open the door to the possibility of restored family relationships.

APOLOGIZING TO PARENTS

A few years ago when my son, Derek, was in graduate school, he lived and worked in a house church in the Haight-Ashbury district of San Francisco. His ministry focused on building relationships with young adults who had migrated to that city hoping for a better life but found themselves homeless. At the end of three years in this ministry, Derek said to me, "Dad, almost every person I've gotten to know on the street is estranged from their parents. Most of them haven't had contact with family for years." I inquired about the kind of family dynamics that had led to such estrangement.

"Many of them were verbally, physically, or sexually abused by their parents," Derek answered. "As soon as they were old enough, they ran away and never looked back. However, others come out of homes that were fairly stable and supportive. But in the teenage years, they got involved in drugs. Their parents tried to help but eventually lost hope and gave up, leaving the young people to fend for themselves."

A Wayward Son

I once spent a week with my son, walking the streets of San Francisco and meeting the people with whom he had built relationships. As I listened to the stories of these young adults, I wondered how many mothers and fathers in a distant city or in a rural town prayed daily that their child would return. I remembered the story that Jesus told about a young man who asked his father if he could have his inheritance while he was young rather than waiting until the death of his father. The father agreed, and the young man left with his pockets full of cash and a tidy sum in his savings account. The young man had followed the philosophy, "Eat, drink, and be merry, for tomorrow we die." In due time, he found himself penniless and took a job feeding pigs in order to sustain himself.[1]

One day he woke up with a memory of home and decided that he would travel home, apologize to his father, and ask if he could work as a hired employee on the family farm. Eventually, he turned his decision into reality and walked the long road back to his father, made his sincere apology, and expressed his desire to work as a hired hand on the farm. To his surprise, the father fully forgave and received him not as a hired hand but as a restored son.[2]

As I looked into the eyes of the young adults on the streets of San Francisco, I wondered how many of them might find reconciliation with parents if only the children would choose to apologize.

Children Who Are Willing to Apologize First

To be sure, those who were abused by parents needed also to receive an apology. But that was not likely to happen unless they initiated the process. Parents cannot apologize to an adult child with whom there is no contact. I remembered the story of Marcie, whom I met at a marriage seminar in a Midwestern town. She had been sexually abused by her father; this had greatly affected her sexual relationship with her husband. At the urging of her husband, she went for counseling and soon gained insight into what had happened. Marcie decided to confront her father and deal with what had taken place so long ago. She knew that she did not cause the problem, but she also knew that for many years she had allowed bitterness and anger to keep her from seeking reconciliation with her parents. She had not seen them in many years.

With the help of her counselor and the support of her husband, Marcie called her parents and asked if she could come and see them. They agreed.

Marcie called it "the longest journey I've ever made and the most difficult conversation I've ever had. At the time I knew nothing about the five languages of an apology," she said, "but I knew that I wanted to begin with an apology. In retrospect, I guess I tried to speak all five languages."

Marcie recalls what she said: "I've come to apologize for allowing anger, bitterness, and resentment to keep me away from you for all these years. I know that I was wrong to have done that. I am deeply sorry that we have lost all these years. I don't know if there is anything I can do to make that up to you, but I'm willing to try. I want the future to be different, and I've come to ask you if you will please forgive me."

By the end of her statement, both of her parents were crying. "My mother hugged me first, and then my father hugged me and said, 'Yes. Yes.' I was not prepared for what happened next. My father said, with tears in his eyes, 'I'll forgive you, but first I've got a lot of things that I need to ask you to forgive me for. I know that what I did to you was wrong. I've never discussed this with your mother, but I guess this is the time she needs to know that I abused you in an awful way. Since I've become a Christian, I've asked God to forgive me many times and I've shed many tears. And I hope that your mother can forgive me too.'

"I hugged my father and said, 'I do forgive you. I'm a Christian too, and I know that Christ died for your sins as well as mine.'

"My mother looked at my dad and said, 'I don't know if I can forgive you; to think that this is what kept my baby away from me all these years.'

"We spent the next two hours talking and crying together. I encouraged my parents to see a counselor so they could work through the emotions this had created. It was the beginning of a healing journey for all of us."

I must state clearly that, in my opinion, if her father had not apologized for his offense, the relationship would not have been restored. Marcie could not have apologized for her father; only he could do that. In her apology, she was dealing with her own failures; that is all any of us can do. But often, our willingness to apologize creates an emotional climate that makes it easier for the other person to apologize. I wondered how many of the young adults with whom I spoke on the streets of San Francisco might find a similar reunion if they chose to walk the road of apologizing.

APOLOGIZING TO YOUR ADULT CHILDREN

Now, let's look at the other side of the equation. There are no perfect parents. We have seen young adults accept their parents' apologies and genuinely forgive them for serious abuses. If you have an estranged relationship with your young adult child, why not take the initiative to apologize? Think of the years of pain that could have been avoided if Marcie's father had taken the initiative to confess his wrong and seek forgiveness years earlier. His embarrassment would have been a small price to pay for the emotional healing, and his asking forgiveness could have alleviated years of estrangement. Not all failures are as devastating as sexual abuse, but when we wrong our children, the results are always negative. Admitting our failures and asking our young adults to forgive us is the road to removing emotional barriers.

Recognize a Strained Relationship

Typically, the wrongs we have committed are not moral but rather relational. During one single-adult conference I spoke on the child/parent relationship. Afterward, Brenda came to me and asked, "May I tell you my story?" "Certainly," I said.

"My parents are good people," she began. "They have done much for me. In fact, that's the problem. They have done too much for me. I'm an only child, and they both devoted their lives to me. Their philosophy was 'Let me do it for you.' Consequently, I grew up with the feeling that I was not capable of doing anything. I remember that once when I was about seven, I made up my own bed that morning. My mother came in a few minutes later and said, 'Oh, my. What a mess,' and she proceeded to make up the bed her way. I guess she thought she was doing the right thing, but it fostered in me a spirit of inadequacy. I didn't do well in college, largely because of my self-concept."

"I love my parents deeply," Brenda continued. "I think that their marriage was so insecure that they both found their only satisfaction in taking care of my needs. I wish they had taken care of each other and let me learn to take care of myself. I wish I could tell them what I feel, but I don't want to hurt them. Mom wonders why I don't come home more often."

I was extremely empathetic with Brenda. I have met many young adults who struggle with similar parental patterns. The parents are typically hardworking people who may have grown up with little. Their hard work has made them successful, and they want to do for their children what was not done for them. However, they do so much that their children never learn to do for themselves. Their "kindness" fosters a dependence that appears in several areas of life, the most obvious of which is financial. The young adult grows up knowing little about the value of money and feeling low motivation to work. Not only is the young adult financially handicapped, but he or she also has relational and emotional struggles.

If you are the parent of an adult child with whom you have a strained relationship or who in your opinion is underperforming in various areas of life, you may want to reflect upon your parenting patterns. It may be time for an apology.

Apologize Even When the Offense Is Unintended

It's not that you intentionally made mistakes. You were trying to care for your child. However, your behavior has made life more difficult for your son or daughter. Your apology cannot undo the emotional and relational inadequacies of your young adult, but it may well bring healing to your relationship. The fact that you are now seeing what the young adult has seen for many years but has been unwilling to share with you communicates to him or her that you are sensitive to your own failures and have the courage to admit them.

If you know the primary apology language of your young adult, be sure and include that in your apology. If you do not, then our suggestion is that you speak all five apology languages, and you are bound to hit it.

For example, if your young adult's primary apology language is *accepting responsibility*—i.e., what they want to hear is "I was wrong," and you leave this out of your apology—you may find that it does not have the desired results of reconciliation. A sincere apology opens up the possibility of forgiveness and true reconciliation.

APOLOGIZING TO BROTHERS AND SISTERS

Most siblings, in the process of growing up, do and say things that are hurtful to each other. If they were not taught to apologize, these hurts may become emotional barriers in their relationship. I remember Michael's visit to my counseling office. "I became a Christian about two years ago . . . but something really troubles me. My brother and I have a really poor relationship; in fact, I haven't spoken with him in five years. Since my mother's funeral, I haven't bothered to talk to him."

An Argument about a Tombstone

"So what happened to set this off?" I asked.

"Well, after the funeral my sister and I were talking with him about a tombstone for Mom's grave. He said he didn't believe in tombstones, that it was a waste of money. I got really angry with him and told him that if that was the way he felt, I didn't care to ever see him again. So my sister and I paid for the tombstone, and I haven't seen him since. It didn't bother me so much until I became a

Christian, and I've been reading the Bible about forgiveness. And I think it is not right for me to hold that against him."

"What kind of relationship did you and your brother have before your mother's funeral?" I asked.

"We got along fairly well," he said. "I wouldn't say we were super close, but we never had any words with each other. We both respected each other. He didn't come to see Mom as much as I wished. I went by every day to see her; my sister saw her almost as often. But he came by maybe once a week. I guess the tombstone thing was just the straw that broke the camel's back."

"What about your father?" I inquired.

"He left us when we were all young. I haven't seen him in years. Mom never remarried. She spent all of her energy working and trying to keep food on the table for us. I guess that's another reason I resent my brother's attitude."

"It's not hard for me to understand how that would upset you," I said. "I would probably be upset myself in that situation. But I think you would probably agree that you overreacted when you told him that you never wanted to see him again."

"I know," he said. "I was just so angry; that's the way I felt at the moment. But I know that I need to try to make it right. It's not right for brothers to live in the same town and not talk to each other."

"Have you ever heard your brother apologize to you for anything in the past?" I asked.

He thought for a moment and said, "I can't remember ever hearing him apologize to me. He did tell my sister that he was sorry that he didn't visit Mother more when she was sick. I was glad to hear that, but it was too late then."

I explained to Michael the languages of an apology and told him why I asked him if he had ever heard his brother apologize. "Typically, people speak the apology language they desire to receive," I explained. "Since he said to your sister that he was sorry that he didn't visit your mother more often when she was sick, I'm guessing that his apology language is *expressing regret*: 'I'm sorry. I feel bad about what I did.'"

'I've Really Missed You'

"Therefore, what I'm going to suggest is that you contact your brother and offer him an apology for the way you spoke to him and what you said to him about your mother's tombstone."

"That's going to be hard," he said.

"You are right. Probably one of the hardest things you've ever done in your life," I affirmed, "but perhaps one of the most productive." Together we worked on a possible apology statement. It looked something like this:

> I realize that I overreacted to you after Mother's funeral when we were talking about the tombstone. I feel bad about having said what I said to you. I know it was wrong, and I've thought a lot about it since then. I really am sorry that I said that. I don't know if you can forgive me, but I would like to ask you to forgive me. If there is anything I can do to make it up to you, I'd like to do it. I just feel bad that I've treated you that way and told you that I didn't want to see you again. I've really missed you. I know I can't take back the words, but I do want to say that I am sorry that I ever said those words. That's not really what I desire, and I hope that you can forgive me.

Michael read the apology aloud, and tears came to his eyes. "That's really the way I feel," he said. "I'd like an opportunity to say this to him. How do I go about it?" he asked.

"I suggest you call him on the phone and ask him if you could come by and see him for a few minutes one evening. If he says no, then I suggest you wait a month and call him again. But I have an idea that he may say yes. If so, when you arrive at his house, don't spend a lot of time in small talk. Get right to the point and let him know that you've come to apologize to him for something that has been bothering you for a long time. After you've seen your brother, I'd like for you to give me a call, because I'd like to know how it went." He agreed and thanked me for our time together.

His Brother's Response
Six weeks later, I got a call from Michael, asking for a follow-up appointment.

"Great. I'd like to hear it."

A couple of days later Michael came to my office. "I can't tell you how glad I am that I took your advice," he said. "It was one of the most difficult things I've ever done in my life, but when I apologized to my brother, he started crying. He said, 'I know what I said was wrong. I should have helped pay for Mom's tombstone. I don't know; I've never been much for sentimental things. But I know it was wrong. At first I was hurt and angry with your response. But later I realized that you had a right to say what you said. I probably would have said the same thing if I had been in your shoes. So I guess what I'm saying is I will forgive you if you will forgive me.'

"We hugged each other, and both of us cried for a long time. And then my brother said, 'I want you to tell me how much the tombstone cost, because I want to pay you and Sis for my part.'

"'You don't need to do that,' I said. 'Just the fact that we've gotten back together is enough payment for me.'

"'I know, but I want to do it for my sake and for Mom,' he said with tears running down his face."

"'Okay,' I said. 'I'll try to find the papers and let you know how much it was.' Then we sat down and talked for an hour about what had been going on in our lives since Mom died. It was a wonderful time, and I feel like our relationship has been restored. We're having him and his wife over to our house next week for a cookout. My wife and I are excited to learn what's been going on in their lives. Thanks for giving me the courage to apologize," he said.

Few Things More Powerful

"I'm glad you followed through," I said. "Few things are more powerful in human relationships than learning to accept responsibility for failures and to sincerely apologize to the person we have wronged."

I believe that many sibling relationships could be healed if someone was willing to take the initiative and apologize. I cannot guarantee that all apologies will be as successful in restoring relationships as was Michael's apology, but I can assure you that relationships are always better when someone chooses to apologize.

APOLOGIZING TO YOUR SPOUSE

The marital relationship is the core relationship in a family. Healthy marriages are characterized by spouses who learn to apologize when they offend each other. Learning to speak the primary apology language of your spouse can make marital apologies much more effective in restoring the relationship.

One sunny afternoon, a young couple arrived in my (Jennifer's) counseling office. Audrey and Chris had one child and had been married for twelve years, although neither looked a day older than thirty. Audrey was the talkative one, so she began to explain the reason they had come. She had recently looked at her computer's history archive and found that Chris (who has flexible work hours) was looking at pornography most days after she went to work. Audrey was very hurt by Chris's actions; yet both were committed to resolving the problem and strengthening their marriage.

I was impressed with the desire of the couple—they showed concern for each other's feelings, and they were both willing to talk about the issues of pornography and marital intimacy. Chris was surprisingly nondefensive. He had already agreed to quit looking at all pornography because it upset Audrey.

For her part, Audrey was encouraged by Chris's compliance, but she longed for something more from Chris. She wanted him to understand her feelings of betrayal, which he said he did not understand. Audrey had used her strong reasoning skills to talk for hours with Chris. How would he feel if the tables were turned and she looked at other men? As we spoke in this session, Audrey was able to share from her heart how she had tried to be all that Chris needed, losing weight and making herself available to Chris without reservation.

In this context Chris began to realize that his involvement in pornography made Audrey feel that she could not satisfy him sexually. It made her feel like a failure. With this insight came a change of attitude for Chris. He was no longer just "sorry" that his habit upset Audrey; he felt that his use of pornography was now "wrong" because it violated his oneness with Audrey.

"I see now how wrong I was," Chris told Audrey in my presence. "I really thought it was a harmless thing, but I see it has the potential of destroying our intimacy. That's the last thing I want to happen."

Audrey breathed a sigh of relief, saying that Chris's change of heart about pornography made his apology more meaningful. It also cleared the way for him to truly set aside pornography out of inner conviction rather than forced compliance—an important difference.

Audrey's primary apology language was accepting responsibility. She wanted to hear Chris say, "I was wrong." All he had been able to do before our counseling session was to say, "I'm sorry I hurt you." That was not enough for Audrey. She didn't see that as a sincere apology, but when he was willing to acknowledge that pornography was wrong, she was ready to forgive him.

Chris and Audrey learned not only the value of an apology but the value of speaking that apology in the language of the spouse. It is this insight that has the potential of bringing reconciliation to thousands of couples. It is our desire that this book will help couples learn how to effectively communicate their sincere apologies.

APOLOGIZING TO YOUR IN-LAWS

In our society, mother-in-law jokes have become so rampant that many people feel reluctant to admit that they have a good relationship with their mother-in-law. On the other hand, a self-centered mother-in-law can be a constant "thorn in the flesh." Let me say that in this section we are talking about fathers-in-law, daughters-in-law, and sons-in-law just as much as we are talking about mothers-in-law. In-law relationships can be difficult to navigate for one basic reason: Marriage brings together two sets of traditions and patterns of family relationships. These differences almost inevitably create conflicts. Failure to deal with these conflicts can create years of "in-law problems."

I (Gary) remember the couple who sat in my office some months ago. "We don't understand our daughter-in-law," said Katherine. "She has told us that she doesn't want us to visit our grandchildren without calling and making sure it is convenient for her. What kind of relationship is that?"

Her husband, Curtis, added: "I grew up in a home where my grandparents stopped by almost every day. It was one of the highlights of my childhood. We like our daughter-in-law. When she was dating Alan, we were pleased when they announced that they were going to get married. But it's like now that they have children, she's changed. Why would she want to make everything so difficult?"

"Probably because she's a wife and mother and employee and a choir member," I said. "And life gets pretty hectic; for you to drop by unexpectedly is another stress factor for her."

I could tell they were shocked at my answer, so I continued talking. "Do she and Alan often ask you to babysit with the children?" I asked.

"Almost every week," Katherine said. "That's the thing about it. We try to help them out so they can have time together, and then she treats us this way."

I tried to explain to them the difference in family dynamics and the difference in generational patterns. "When you were children, life was much simpler, easier, and slower; and neighbors often visited with neighbors. Front porches with rocking chairs were common, but in today's world, porches and rocking chairs are a thing of the past. It's TV, computers, swimming classes, dance classes, piano lessons, Little League, etc. Family life is much busier. For the average family, there is very little leisure time. Consequently, to have in-laws visit whenever it is convenient for them often puts greater stress on the young couple as they seek to rear their children."

I told them that their daughter-in-law's request that they call before coming and make sure it was convenient for them was not abnormal in today's culture. I suggested that Katherine and Curtis make the most of the opportunities they get to babysit with their grandchildren and recognize those times as their primary opportunities for interacting with them.

Then I suggested that they needed to apologize to their daughter-in-law for being insensitive to the stress their unannounced visits were causing. I could tell that this was not the way they had expected this conversation to end. But I could also tell that they were grappling with what I was saying and trying to understand. I commended them for coming to see me and trying to get help rather than letting this simply continue until they ended up doing or saying something very destructive to the in-law relationship.

"You are at a very crucial point in your relationship with your daughter-in-law," I suggested. "I think that a sincere apology from you will mend the hurt and allow you to have a positive relationship in the future. Do you know your daughter-in-law's primary apology language?" I asked. The blank look in their eyes told me that was a new concept. So I explained to them the five languages of apology and why it was important to speak the other person's primary apology language.

"I think her language must be accepting responsibility," Katherine said, "because Alan told us that when they have spats, she wants him to say, 'I was wrong,' and that anything short of that she doesn't consider an apology."

"Then let's assume that is her primary apology language," I said, "so be sure you include that in your apology. It won't hurt to throw in some of the other languages as well." We spent the next few minutes working on a possible apology statement. Here's what we ended up with:

We have realized that our coming by unannounced has put unnecessary pressure on you and Alan and the children. That is certainly not our desire. We realize that has been wrong, and we would like to ask you to forgive us. In both our childhoods, life was a lot different; much slower and people stopped by all the time unannounced. But we know that it's different now. We all live with a lot of pressure. You have work and church and all the children's activities. We certainly want to respect that. We appreciate your letting us babysit the children. We enjoy those times. So feel free to call on us anytime. And we promise we will try not to just stop by but always call to see if it is convenient. And if not, we won't take it personally, because we know how stressful life can be sometimes. We love you two so much, and we want you to have good family relationships and a strong marriage. We want to be an asset and not a liability. So will you forgive us for being a little pushy in the past? We know it was wrong, and we want to make it different in the future.

Later they told me that their apology was successful and they felt that their relationship with their daughter-in-law was now healthy. "I guess we've got to learn to live in the twenty-first century," they said. "Thanks for helping us."

Most troubled in-law relationships could be mended if someone were willing to apologize and learn how to express the apology in the language of the other person.

APOLOGIZING TO AUNTS AND UNCLES

In today's cultural climate of geographically dispersed families, aunts and uncles are often minor players in family relationships. However, if there are opportunities to build relationships with aunts and uncles, the hope would be for positive relationships. If they are to be positive, it means that periodically you may be called upon to apologize.

A childhood friend named Victor told me (Jennifer) a story about the most powerful acceptance of an apology that he had ever received. Almost forty years ago he offended his aunt, but Aunt Annie left an indelible impression on him with her loving spirit when she accepted his apology and forgave him. During his rebellious teenage years, Victor and a friend burglarized his aunt Annie's house. The boys took some cash and liquor; however, Victor stopped his friend from taking any personal items such as his aunt's ring, which was sitting on her dresser.

Many years later, Victor had a spiritual awakening and felt overwhelming remorse about his actions. He wrote a letter of confession and apology to his aunt, and he carried the letter around without mailing it for several weeks. He really hated to admit such a terrible mistake to Aunt Annie, whom he greatly respected. One day he placed the letter in a blue postal box, but even as he released the handle it seemed to stick to his hand with the weight of all his reservations.

Weeks passed, and then Victor received a simple response to his apology. As he recalls it, Aunt Annie wrote, "I always thought it was you because I knew it was someone who loved me, who didn't take my most valuable items. I want you to know that I forgive you freely, and I appreciate your apology." A few weeks later, Victor was able to visit with his now-ill aunt and uncle. They affirmed their forgiveness and their thankfulness that he had been willing to deal with his past failure. He had acted just in time, because six months later, his aunt Annie died. His apology was liberating.

Victor told me that he has often wondered what would have happened if his aunt had died before he apologized. It was something he's glad he did not take with him to his own grave. Apologies hold the potential for deepening relationships, while failure to apologize may hang like a weight around our necks for a lifetime.

APOLOGIZING TO GRANDPARENTS

Most of us think of grandparents as loving, smiling people who do good things for grandchildren. Of course, in reality there are all types of grandparents. Some fit the image of being loving and happy. Others, however, are harsh, self-centered, and cruel. Grandchildren also come in all sizes, shapes, and temperaments. Some are easy to love; others are more difficult because of their obnoxious behavior. Grandchildren can be harsh and cruel as well. Some grandchildren have stolen from grandparents. Others have spoken unkindly about grandparents' prudishness or religious beliefs. Still others ignore and withdraw from grandparents.

There are various occasions on which grandchildren might need to apologize to grandparents for their words or behavior. Understanding the apology language of your grandparents will create the possibility of your apology being more effective and restoring a positive relationship.

At age seventeen, Paula stole her grandparents' car while they were away on vacation, took a joyride, wrecked the car, and ended up in the hospital. Before this event, she had a good relationship with her grandparents. She freely came and went at their house. They had often given her spending money and had showered her with numerous gifts. The grandparents were deeply hurt that Paula had violated their trust. They never dreamed that Paula would take advantage of them in this way. Paula had gone out with friends that night and had been drinking. While under the influence of alcohol she got the idea of taking the joyride. Her friends had tried to talk her out of the idea, but she insisted that her grandparents would not mind.

Two days later when her grandparents returned from their vacation, they visited Paula in the hospital. Physically she was not hurt badly, but emotionally she was a wreck. She knew she had failed two important people who loved her very much. So she apologized profusely.

"I'm so sorry," she said. "I know what I did was wrong. I should not have taken advantage of you. I feel so bad about what I've done. And I'm so sorry that your car is wrecked. I was drinking that night. I shouldn't have been drinking in the first place, but that's no excuse for taking your car. I'm so sorry, and I hope you can forgive me."

Her grandfather said very slowly, "Paula, what you did has disappointed us greatly. We never dreamed that you would do something like this. We didn't even know that you were drinking alcohol, and we're saddened to hear that, because you could have been killed that night. We know you are sorry right now, and we know that you regret what you did. But if you really want to sincerely apologize, then you will have to repay whatever it costs to get the car repaired. Then we'll know that your apology is sincere.

"We love you. We want the best for you, but we cannot overlook what you have done. You must be accountable and suffer the consequences. So whenever you get well, we'll work out a payment schedule. And you can pay us back out of your allowance and your part-time job."

When they left the room, Paula was in a state of shock. She never dreamed that her grandfather would respond that way. She thought he would freely forgive her if she apologized and cried. She did not understand two things. First, her grandfather's apology language was making restitution. To him an apology was not sincere if it did not include making restitution for the wrong that was done. Second, her grandfather knew that if she suffered no consequences for her actions, it would simply be a matter of time until she would be drunk again and do something just as harmful and perhaps worse. He was doing her a great service when he told her that she would have to repay whatever it cost to have the car repaired.

He later admitted that it was one of the hardest statements that he'd ever made, because he loved his granddaughter. He prayed that it would be a lesson she would never forget.

Months later, after Paula had repaid half the cost of the repair, her grandfather said to her, "Paula, you've demonstrated to me that you are a person of integrity. You have been faithful in paying your payments every month for the car. I hope you have learned a big lesson from this. And I am sure in my heart that you will never do anything like that again. So I want you to know that I'm going to forgive the other half of your debt, and you can use your money in some other way because you have demonstrated to me that your apology was sincere and you have accepted responsibility for your actions."

He gave her a big hug; she cried and said, "Thank you, Grandfather. I really appreciate that, and I can tell you it's a lesson I'll never forget. And I don't drink alcohol anymore. I made the decision that, for me, life is more important than alcohol."

"I'm glad to hear that," her grandfather said as he gave her a big hug.

Healthy family relationships require sincere apologies for one reason: All of us fail from time to time. None of us is perfect in relating to our family members. Healthy family relationships do not require perfection, but they do require that we deal with our failures in a positive way. A sincere apology is the most important step in healing offenses and rebuilding relationships.

The FIVE LANGUAGES *of* APOLOGY

EXPRESSING REGRET
"I am sorry"

ACCEPTING RESPONSIBILITY
"I was wrong"

MAKING RESTITUTION
"What can I do to make it right?"

GENUINELY REPENTING
"I'll try not to do that again"

REQUESTING FORGIVENESS
"Will you please forgive me?"

11

Teaching Your CHILD
to Apologize

I recently read three dozen of the most popular books on parenting. None included a single chapter on teaching children to apologize. I thought, *Perhaps I have discovered another reason why adults often find it hard to apologize—they were never taught as children.*

I remembered Robert Fulghum's words in his best-selling book, *All I Really Need to Know I Learned in Kindergarten*: "Say you're sorry when you hurt somebody."[1] Fulghum said that was one of about a dozen things he learned in kindergarten. So I decided to contact some kindergarten teachers to see if they were still teaching this in kindergarten. I discovered that none of these teachers had received a curriculum that deals with the subject of apologizing. If a teacher happens to think that this is important, she may try to teach children to say "I'm sorry." But nothing in the curriculum would encourage this. So if Robert Fulghum were attending kindergarten today, he would probably have one less chapter in his book!

In reflecting, I ask myself why that is no longer a truth for five-year-olds to learn. Is it the amoral climate of contemporary society that accounts for the scarcity of material on teaching children to apologize? Do we fear that we will damage their self-esteem if we require them to admit that their behavior may hurt others? Has our love for freedom and creativity blinded us to the reality that total freedom leads to anarchy? Or is it the philosophy that man is innately good; that the child simply needs a safe environment in which to develop this innate goodness; and if the environment is right, the child will never need to apologize?

Whatever the reason, I think that Robert Fulghum was right, and all of us need to go back to kindergarten.

If adults need to apologize (and who would argue against that?), then the art of apology needs to be learned in childhood. In this chapter we would like to share some ideas that we hope parents will find helpful—things your children need to know.

WHAT CHILDREN NEED TO KNOW:
1. ACCEPT RESPONSIBILITY FOR YOUR ACTIONS

The first step in teaching our sons and daughters to apologize is to lead them to accept responsibility for their own behavior. This can begin very early and in morally neutral settings.

Our adult patterns of sweeping issues under the rug and shifting blame can often be traced all the way back to childhood habits. As a very innocent example, I (Jennifer) heard a two-year-old child pass gas and then blame it on his diaper: "My diaper burped!"

My sister and brother-in-law inadvertently reminded me of the value of helping children accept responsibility for their actions at an early age. Elisabeth and Bill had come to visit us in Baltimore. I remember riding in the car together. Their first child, Anna, was only two years old at the time. As we drove along on an errand, Anna studied a potato chip that I had given her, gripped it tightly in her tiny fingers, and quickly snapped the chip into two pieces. Anna exclaimed, "It broke!"

"No, Anna. You broke the chip," Bill responded.

Redirected but not bothered, Anna quickly corrected her statement: "I broke it."

I noted this minor correction with interest and filed it away as a good example of how to start early and gently in teaching children to "own up" to their actions. The broken chip has nothing to do with morality but everything to do with helping a child learn to accept responsibility for her behavior.

I (Gary) mentioned earlier our son's classic statement: "It did it by itself." When the glass lay broken on the floor, he would say, "It did it by itself." When the wall was marked with Magic Marker, again he would say, "It did it by itself." We worked long and hard at getting him to say, "I accidentally knocked the glass off the table" and "I marked on the wall."

Accepting responsibility for one's words and actions is the first step in learning to apologize. Typically children easily accept responsibility for their positive actions. "I ate three bites of my beans; may I have dessert?" "I ran the fastest." "I got a smiley face on my paper." "I painted this in art class." These are all statements accepting responsibility for noble deeds done.

On the other hand, children are not as quick to accept responsibility for deeds that are not so noble. When is the last time you heard a three-year-old admit, "I ate the cookie that Mommy told me not to eat"? Or, "I pushed Nicole down the steps"? This level of accepting responsibility takes far more parental effort.

One way to help children learn to accept responsibility for their not-so-noble deeds is to help them rephrase their statements, beginning the sentence with "I." Andy had left the door open, and a stray cat had come into the house. When his mother asked, "How did this cat get in the house?" Andy responded, "She just showed up. I guess she came down the chimney."

"Let's try that again," his mother said. "Repeat this sentence, 'I opened the door and the cat came in the house.'"

So Andrew said, "I opened the door and came in the house and there was this cat looking at me." He looked at his mother and smiled.

"Try it once more," his mother said. "Repeat after me: 'I opened the door and came into the house.'"

"I opened the door and came in the house," Andrew repeated.

"And who didn't close the door?" his mother continued.

"The cat didn't close the door," Andrew said, laughing.

"That's true," his mom said. "But who really didn't close the door?"

"I didn't close the door."

"Yes," his mother said. "When we start our sentences with 'I,' we are being responsible for our actions. Now help me get this cat out of the house. I'll get some milk, and you open the door, and maybe the cat will follow us outside."

Mom is having fun and yet teaching Andrew how to accept responsibility for his actions.

WHAT CHILDREN NEED TO KNOW:
2. YOUR ACTIONS AFFECT OTHERS

The second step in teaching children how to apologize is to help them understand that their actions always affect others. If I help my mother set the table, my mother feels happy. If I throw the football inside the house and break the lamp, my mother feels sad. If I say to my father, "I love you," my father feels loved. If I say to him, "I hate you," my father feels hurt. My words and my actions either help people or hurt people. When I help people, I feel good about myself. When I hurt people, I feel bad.

There is a golden rule in life that says to treat others the way you would like them to treat you. Every child needs to learn the Golden Rule.[2] It sets the standard for learning how to treat others. It also communicates to the mind of a child that some things are good and some things are bad, and I should aspire to do what is good.

Life affords many opportunities to teach children that our actions affect others. Hillary is six years old and in the first grade. Her brother, Daniel, is four years old and attends preschool. One afternoon before dinner, they were playing together when her mother heard Hillary say to Daniel, "You are a barbarian. Get out of my room." Daniel burst into tears and ran to his mom. "Hillary called me a barbarian."

His mother gave him a big hug and said, "I know. I will have to talk to her about that. Why don't you sit here and color in your book while I talk with Hillary?" Her mother walked to Hillary's room and said, "Honey, where did you hear the word *barbarian?*"

"At school," she said. "Brad called Ethan a barbarian."

"Do you know what that word means?"

"It's a person who does something bad," she said.

"That's right," her mother said. "But it's not nice to call people names."

"But Daniel did something bad. He messed up my dollhouse. I had it all arranged, and he knocked it all over."

"You're right. That's not a nice thing to do," her mother said. "And Daniel needs to say 'I'm sorry.' But it wasn't very nice to call him a barbarian either. He was very hurt that you called him a bad name. So I think you need to say 'I'm sorry' also."

Mother walked into the kitchen and took Daniel by the hand and said, "I want to talk to you and Hillary. Come with me. I think that both of you know that what you did was wrong. Daniel, when Hillary is playing with her dollhouse, it's wrong for you to come in and mess it up. Do you understand that?" Daniel nodded yes. "It made Hillary feel very upset because she had worked hard to arrange her dollhouse. And, Hillary, when you called Daniel a barbarian, it hurt him very much. You heard him cry and cry because he was hurt so badly. When we do bad things and when we call people names, we hurt them very deeply. And when we hurt someone, we need to say 'I'm sorry.'

"Hillary, since you are the oldest, I think you should go first."

Hillary paused and then said, "I'm sorry I called you a barbarian."

"Now it's your turn, Daniel," his mother said.

"I'm sorry," he said.

"Sorry for what?" his mother prodded.

"I'm sorry I messed up your dollhouse," he said.

"Good. Now give each other a hug," Mom suggested. They hugged each other and Mom said, "Good. Now Daniel, you go finish coloring and, Hillary, you play in your room. I'll call you both when dinner is ready."

This mother has her own kindergarten and is clearly teaching her children that our actions affect other people. And when we do wrong, we need to say "I'm sorry."

WHAT CHILDREN NEED TO KNOW:
3. THERE ARE ALWAYS RULES IN LIFE

A third step in teaching children to apologize is helping them understand that there are always rules in life. The most important rule is the Golden Rule—treat others the way you would like for them to treat you. But there are other rules—many rules—and most of them are designed to help us have a good life. "We don't throw the football inside the house" is a rule most parents have made for obvious reasons. "We don't take something that doesn't belong to us. We don't tell things that are untrue about others. We don't cross the street without looking both ways. We say 'thank you' when someone gives us something or says something nice about us. We go to school every day, Monday through Friday, unless we are sick."

There are hundreds of rules for children. Some of them are made by parents, others by schoolteachers, and still others by grandparents. Almost always, these rules are designed to help the child have a healthy childhood and grow to become a responsible adult.

For adults, there are many more rules. Some are self-imposed, such as "I will go to the gym three mornings a week until I've lost twenty pounds." Some are mutually agreed upon between husband and wife, such as "We will keep each other informed about our schedules." Other rules are made by the government, and still others are handed down by God. Without rules, life would be chaotic.

What Rules—and Why?

When parents set rules for children, the overarching question should be: "Is this rule good for my child? Will it have some positive effect on the child's life?" Here are some practical questions to ask as you decide about a particular rule:

- Does this rule keep the child from danger or destruction?
- Does this rule teach the child some positive character trait: honesty, hard work, kindness, sharing, and more?
- Does this rule protect property?
- Does this rule teach the child responsibility?
- Does this rule teach good manners?

In answering questions like these, we are far more likely to come up with healthy rules for the family. These are the factors about which we are concerned as parents. We want to keep our children from danger and destruction. We do not want our young child to be hit by a car in the street, and we do not want our older children to get involved in drugs. We want to teach our children positive character traits in keeping with our values. We want children to respect the property of others; thus, a rule about not playing baseball in the backyard may well keep them from breaking a neighbor's window. We want them to learn to take care of their own possessions; thus, a rule about putting the bicycle in the storage shed at night is a purposeful rule.

We want our children to be responsible adults, and we know that they must learn this in childhood. Therefore, requiring a child to be responsible for making his bed or vacuuming his floor is a responsible rule. And what of good manners? It is interesting that contemporary corporate executives are hiring etiquette trainers and consultants because the social graces of contemporary employees are so greatly characterized by rudeness and crudeness. I believe this can be traced to the lack of teaching manners in the home. If a parent believes that "please" and "thank you" are better than "gimme" and "yuck," then there will be rules regarding such manners in the home.

Once parents have agreed on a rule, the entire family needs to be made aware of it. Unspoken rules are unfair rules. A child cannot be expected to live up to a standard of which he is unaware. Parents have the responsibility for making sure that children understand what the rules are. As children grow older, they need to know why their parents have decided on this rule. If children feel genuinely loved by the parents, they will usually acknowledge the value of such rules.

Rules Can Change

Good family rules are not set in concrete. If you come to see that a particular rule is detrimental rather than helpful, then you should be willing to change that rule. In our family, we started out with the rule of no singing at the table. We quickly realized that this rule was a product of our families of origin and did not fit our view of what a mealtime should be. With my wife being a musician and me having a deep appreciation for music, we quickly concluded that that rule needed to be abandoned and that anyone who wanted to break forth in song at our table was welcomed to do so (as long as there was no food in the person's mouth).

And If a Rule Is Broken . . .

With the rules come consequences when the rules are broken. The sign by the roadside said "$100 Fine for Littering." I took my candy wrapper and tucked it under the floor mat. I didn't have $100 I wanted to give the city. The litter that lines our highways is testimony that consequences do not motivate everyone to obedience.

Nor are consequences the only thing that motivates us to obedience. Having an aesthetic eye, I have always enjoyed driving down a highway uncluttered with cans, bags, and plastic bottles. Therefore, my appreciation for beauty motivates me to hold on to my candy wrapper, but I must admit that an awareness of the $100 fine also adds to my motivation.

The breaking of civil rules usually brings negative consequences. One of the difficulties of our society is that in recent years the consequences of doing wrong have been delayed by long and tedious court proceedings. And on many occasions, the consequences have been minimal. I believe that this has contributed to the growth of civil misconduct over the past twenty-five years. Effective motivation to civil obedience requires quick and certain consequences.

In the family, the principle is the same. Obedience is learned by suffering the consequences of disobedience. Effective teaching of obedience requires that consequences for breaking rules should cause discomfort to the rule breaker. The child who has to pay for breaking the lamp that was broken by the football thrown inside the house will think twice before he throws the football again.

Consequences should be as closely associated with the rule as possible. For example, if a sixteen-year-old is found speeding, then he loses the privilege of driving for a week. A second offense would be the loss of driving privileges for perhaps two weeks. Not many teenagers will get beyond those two weeks!

It is ideal if the consequences for breaking family rules can be determined and discussed with the family at the time the rule is made. This has the advantage of the child knowing ahead of time what the consequences will be. And it delivers the parents from the peril of having to make a snap judgment about what discipline should be applied. Deciding the consequences before the child breaks the rule is also more likely to give you a reasonable consequence.

Enforce the Rules

Once the rules have been clearly defined and the consequences of misbehavior have been communicated, it is the parents' responsibility to make sure the child experiences the consequences of his misbehavior. When parents are permissive one day and let misbehavior slide, and the next day come down hard on the child for the same misbehavior, the parents are on the sure road of rearing a disobedient, disrespectful child. Inconsistent discipline is the most common pitfall of parents who are trying to raise responsible children. The consequences should be brought to bear as quickly after the disobedience has occurred as possible. Always the discipline must be administered with love and firmness.

Having the consequences for misbehavior set in advance keeps you from being controlled by your emotional state at the moment. If you have already agreed on what the consequences will be, your responsibility is simply to see that those consequences are carried out. You don't have to decide what will be done; you simply decide to follow through with what you have agreed will be done. You are not as likely to yell and scream or physically be excessive with your children because of your own emotional state if you have already decided on the consequences.

Discipline must always be done in a spirit of love with the parent in full control of his/her emotions, never accompanied with screaming and yelling, but always accompanied with deep sympathy for the child's pain. The child should realize that the parent also regrets that playing in the big game will not happen, but that is the reality of life. When one person disobeys, others inevitably suffer. It is through their suffering that children learn obedience and through consistency that parents earn the right to be honored.

Few things are more important in teaching a child to apologize than establishing clear, meaningful rules, consequences when the rules are broken, and fairly and firmly administering the consequences when necessary. This process establishes in the mind of the child that "I am responsible for my words and my actions; that when I follow the rules, I reap the benefits, and when I choose to break the rules, I suffer the consequences." It develops a sense of morality: Some things are right, and some things are wrong. When I do right, there are good results. When I do wrong, there are negative results. It is this sense of morality that helps the child understand the need for an apology.

WHAT CHILDREN NEED TO KNOW:
4. APOLOGIES WILL RESTORE FRIENDSHIPS

The fourth step in helping children learn to apologize is helping them understand that apologies are necessary in order to maintain good relationships. When I hurt other people by my words or my behavior, I have established a barrier between that person and me. If I don't learn to apologize, the barrier will remain and my relationship with that person will be fractured. My hurtful words or actions push people away from me, and without apology, they continue to walk away. The child, teenager, or adult who does not learn this reality will eventually end up isolated and alone.

With the help of his mother, Steven is learning this principle. He walked into the house one afternoon, flipped on the TV, and stretched out on the floor. "Why did you come in so early?" his mother, Sharon, asked. "You guys just started playing in the backyard."

"The other boys went home," he answered.

"Why did they go home? It's only four o'clock," Sharon repeated.

"They just went home," he said. His mother sensed that something more was going on, so she asked, "Did something happen that caused the boys to go home early?"

"They didn't want to play the new game," he said. "I'm tired of playing the same old games."

"So what did you tell them?" his mother inquired.

"I told them that if they didn't want to play the new game, they could just go home," Steven said. "So they just went home. It's OK. I was tired of playing anyway. I'd rather watch TV."

Sharon knew that her son had a lesson to learn, but she wisely perceived that this was not the time to teach him a lesson. She said, "I'll have dinner ready in about an hour. You can watch a little TV, and then you need to get started on your homework." She walked back to the kitchen wondering how she would teach her son that he can't always have it his way if he wants to have friends. She realized that was in part why she and Steven's father were divorced: He always insisted on having it his way.

An Empty Backyard

The next afternoon when Sharon arrived home from work, she noticed that the neighborhood boys were not playing in the yard. When she walked into the house, Steven was again stretched out on the floor in front of the TV. "Are you guys not going to play this afternoon?" she asked. "The guys didn't show up," Steven said. "I think they are playing at the park. I didn't want to go down there."

"I'm going to order in pizza tonight," she said. "What would you like on it?"

"Pepperoni and mushrooms with extra cheese," Steven said.

As they ate their pizza, Sharon prayed for wisdom. "I want to talk about what happened yesterday," she said. "Tell me again what you said to the boys."

"I told you last night . . . I wanted them to play a new game, one

I learned at school. But they weren't interested. They wanted to play the same old thing. I like new things; I don't want to play the same games every afternoon."

"So what did you tell them?" his mother asked.

"I told them that if they didn't want to play a new game, then they could go home, because I was tired of playing their games."

"Did you see any of the guys at school today?" his mother asked.

"I saw Austin down the hall," he said, "but he didn't see me."

"So none of the guys talked with you today, and none of them came over this afternoon?"

"Nope," he answered.

"Steven, I know you feel bad about this, because I know how much you enjoy playing. I appreciate the fact that you like to try new games, but what you said to the guys was pretty harsh."

"I didn't think they would really leave," Steven said. "I didn't even realize what I had said until they all walked away. I'm afraid now they're never going to come back and I don't have anybody to play with." Tears were forming in Steven's eyes.

Sharon's heart was broken. She wanted to take him and hold him in her arms, but she knew that would not solve his problem. So she continued. "I'm going to give you a suggestion, and I know it is going to be hard to do it. I think you need to apologize to Austin and the other guys. Tell them that you are sorry you got angry and told them to go home, that you have felt bad about it ever since, and ask them to forgive you."

"But, Mom, they will think I am a wimp," he said.

"What they think is unimportant. What is important is what you know in your heart, and you know that you spoke those words in anger. I don't know whether they will forgive you. And I don't know if they will come back and be friends and you can play again. But I know that unless you apologize, they are not likely to come back. All of us get angry sometimes," she said, "and we sometimes say things that we later regret. But if we are willing to apologize, people will usually forgive us. You know, I've had to apologize to you, and you've had to apologize to me. Apologizing is a very mature thing to do. I know it will be hard, but I think you are man enough to do it."

"Well, I know you're right, Mom, but it's so hard," her son said.

"I know," Sharon said. "But it is a part of growing up, and it's a part of having friends."

A Walk to the Park

After dinner, Steven said, "I'm going to walk down to the park, Mom, and see if the guys are there."

"OK," she said. "Be sure to take your cell phone. Call me if you need me." He nodded and walked out the door. Sharon began to pray again. She knew that Steven was about to do one of the hardest things he had done. But she also knew that if he had the courage to apologize, he was well on the way to becoming a man.

After an hour, Sharon could hardly contain herself. She wondered how things were going. On the pretext of going to the store to get some milk, she drove by the park and saw Steven playing with Austin and the other guys. She was relieved and returned home.

An hour later, Steven came in the house hot and sweaty. "How did it go?" his mom inquired.

"Cool. The guys were really cool. They said we all get mad sometimes and that it was OK. They asked me to play with them, and we had a good time. I told them we could play in our yard tomorrow."

"Great," his mother said. "Steven, I'm so proud of you. Those guys are fortunate to have a friend like you, and I'm fortunate to have a son like you."

The next afternoon, Sharon came home to find the neighborhood guys playing in the backyard. She breathed a sigh of relief and thanked God that it had gone well.

Children must learn that friendships require honest apologies when we realize we have hurt our friends. The child who learns early that apologies restore friendships has learned one of the major lessons about human relationships.

WHAT CHILDREN NEED TO KNOW:
5. LEARN TO SPEAK THE LANGUAGES OF APOLOGY

A final step in teaching children how to apologize is to teach them how to speak the five languages of an apology. Review the list of the five apology languages at the front of this chapter. Remember, the goal is that children will not only know the five languages of an apology but feel comfortable speaking them.

The level of proficiency should increase with age. It is very similar to the developmental process in learning to speak a language. Children begin with words that they associate with certain objects: book, shoe, foot. Then they learn words that are associated with ideas: yes, no. Later they learn to understand sentences such as: "Let's go. Let's put the dress on." Then they learn to speak sentences such as: "I don't like beans. I want to play." It is much later that they learn grammatical rules and complex sentence structure. The child's vocabulary and level of comprehension increase year by year. The same is true in teaching children to speak the apology languages.

A two-year-old can learn to say "I'm sorry" when she pulls the hair of her older sister. Or he could say, "I was wrong. I disobeyed," when he willfully knocks his sippy cup from the table to the floor. Thus, they are learning on the simplest level how to express regret and accept responsibility for their actions.

When the three-year-old pushes her brother down the stairs and he lies in a puddle of tears, the mother may comfort the fallen soldier and teach the three-year-old to say, "I was wrong. I am sorry." And she might even encourage the offender to "go get a Band-Aid for your brother" or say to him, "Let me get the sand off your leg." With running for the Band-Aid or brushing the sand off the leg, the child is learning to make restitution. Also at a very young age, children can learn to say, "I'll try not to do that again. Will you please forgive me?" and in so doing, they are learning the language of genuinely repenting and requesting forgiveness.

The child's level of comprehension and understanding of why we apologize when we hurt someone will increase with age. When the child is six, her apologies will be much more meaningful, because your daughter has a deeper level of understanding that some things are right and some things are wrong. And when we do wrong, we hurt people; and we apologize so that they will feel better. We hope they will forgive us and we can continue to be friends.

Starting Early

In essence, we are saying that a child can learn the vocabulary of an apology rather young. His or her level of comprehension and understanding the importance of an apology grows as he or she gets older. Learning to verbalize the five languages of an apology at an early age lays the foundation for the child's moral and relational development in the later years. One of the reasons that many adults have difficulty learning to speak the languages of an apology is that they never learned the vocabulary in childhood.

In early childhood (ages two through six), the child can learn to verbalize all five languages of an apology. During these early years, the motivation for apologizing is primarily external; that is, the parents are insisting that the child say "I'm sorry" or "I was wrong" or "I disobeyed." This is done in much the same way as we teach children to say "Thank you," "You're welcome," and "Please." The method is repetition, expectation, and, sometimes, the withholding of privileges if the proper word is not spoken. The child learns primarily by outside prompting.

From grade one through grade twelve, the child learns to internalize these concepts and to speak these words from his or her own heart.

What parent does not take pride when she hears her child say without prompting, "Thank you," "Please," and "You're welcome"? Similarly, the parent knows that her teaching is being effective when she hears a child use one or more of the apology languages without being prompted by the parent. I shall always remember the night my teenage son said to me, "I'm sorry, Dad. I was wrong. I should not have yelled at you. I hope that you will forgive me." Of course I did and shared with my wife the good news that apparently our hard work at trying to teach him to apologize was paying real dividends. I knew that if he could say those words to his father, then he would someday be able to say them to his wife and perhaps to his own children.

The Power of Modeling

This leads me to observe that the most powerful method of teaching older children to speak the languages of apology is by your own model. When parents apologize to their children for harsh words or unfair treatment, they are doing their most effective teaching. Young children do what parents say; older children do what parents do.

The parent who reasons, "I don't want to apologize to my children because they will lose respect for me," is greatly deluded. The fact is the parent who sincerely apologizes to a child has just increased the child's respect for the parent. The child knows that what the parent did was wrong. The offense sits as a barrier between the parent and child. When the parent apologizes, the child is typically ready to forgive and the barrier is removed. Some of our finest moments are when we apologize to our children.

'Dad, I'm Proud of You'

Another powerful method of teaching your children to speak the languages of apology is when you apologize to others and share with your children what you have done. I remember the father who said to me, "I had had an altercation with one of my coworkers. And in the process of our disagreement, I had lashed out at him in anger and said some rather harsh things. That night when I got home, I felt terrible. I realized that I had blown it. I shared it with my wife and asked her to pray for me that I would have the courage to apologize the next day. She did, and I did.

"On Friday evening of that week when we had our family conference, I shared with my two children what I had done, both in losing my temper and then in apologizing. When I finished, my ten-year-old son looked at me and said, 'Dad, I'm proud of you. Most men would not go back and apologize.'

"'Thank you, Jonathan,' I said. 'I have to admit it was really hard to apologize, but I knew it was the right thing.'

"Later," he said, "my wife and I talked about how glad we were that I had chosen to share that with the children. We both realized what a positive impact it had upon them." I wish every father had the wisdom and courage to follow the example of this father.

If parents learn to apologize to each other, to their children, and to others, then children will also learn how to speak the languages of apology. If we could have a widespread renewal of the practice of apologizing, imagine the impact it would have on our culture. In fact, we will consider that healing impact more fully in the final chapter, which is entitled "What If We All Learned to Apologize Effectively?"

The FIVE LANGUAGES
of APOLOGY

EXPRESSING REGRET
"I am sorry"

ACCEPTING RESPONSIBILITY
"I was wrong"

MAKING RESTITUTION
"What can I do to make it right?"

GENUINELY REPENTING
"I'll try not to do that again"

REQUESTING FORGIVENESS
"Will you please forgive me?"

12

APOLOGIZING *in* *Dating* Relationships

Dating has been called America's favorite sport for single adults. "Who are you dating?" is a common question when singles get together. Whatever else we say about dating, it is a *relationship* sport. In most sports the emphasis is on winning, which means that someone else must lose. However, in dating, the objective is that we will both enjoy the experience; we will both be winners. When this does not happen, the relationship is short-lived.

Lindsay is twenty-three years old and has just broken up with Zack, whom she had been dating for nine months. "I broke it off because he embarrassed me so many times by being late to events, or not showing up at all. I can't spend my life sitting around waiting for him. When we are together, he is lots of fun. I enjoy being with him, but it's just not worth it." Clearly the relationship causes Lindsay more frustration than pleasure, so she is off to seek a new friendship.

What many couples do not realize and seldom discuss while dating is that apologizing is also an indicator of the health of a relationship. In healthy relationships, the person who offends sincerely apologizes. The offended person graciously forgives, and the relationship proceeds. In an unhealthy relationship, the offender does not apologize or apologizes inadequately, and the offense sits as a silent barrier to their growth. (That's what happened with Lindsay.) With enough barriers, the relationship ends when the offended party decides "enough is enough."

When Lindsay broke up with Zack, it was because his apologies —"I'm sorry. I got detained at the office," or "I'm sorry. The traffic was horrendous" —seemed to her like lame excuses, not apologies. Her primary apology language was "genuine repentance." Zack never even expressed a desire to change. So eventually Lindsay gave up on the relationship.

Many dating relationships end prematurely because one or both parties fail to effectively apologize.

Of course, many who date are looking for more than a solid relationship, as beneficial as that is. They are seeking a "soul mate," someone to spend their life with, and the couple may soon think and talk about marriage. While the purpose of dating is broader than "finding a mate," almost no one in Western society gets married without having first dated.

MOVING BEYOND THE FEELINGS

The big question in deciding to marry someone seems to be, "Are we really in love?" The premise is that if we really love each other, then marriage will bring us the happiness we seek. This "love," however, is usually defined in terms of romantic emotions. One definition is "Love is the feeling that you feel when you feel a feeling like you have never felt before." In an earlier book, *The Five Love Languages for Singles*, I addressed this issue and tried to help singles get a better understanding of the temporary nature of the "in love" emotional experience.[1] I discussed how to make the bridge from being "in love" to the more intentional stage of "choosing to love," and thus keep emotional love alive in a relationship.

I will not repeat that material here, except to say that if the couple does not learn to speak each other's love language, the emotional love will die. Their differences will emerge, and they will find themselves wondering why they got married in the first place. If they learn to speak the right love language, they can keep emotional love alive for a lifetime.

'I CAN'T TAKE ANY MORE PAIN'

Why is it important to learn the five languages of an apology and speak them in a dating relationship? First, because it is the only way to effectively deal with the problem of our imperfect humanity. If you date long enough, you will eventually offend your dating partner by the way you speak or behave. There are no exceptions to this reality. Sincerely apologizing is the best way to deal with these offenses. Unresolved offenses often lead to the eventual breakup of dating relationships.

Chad and Nina had been dating for two years when Nina said, "Chad, I think it's time that we go our separate ways. Our relationship has become too painful to continue."

The next week, I saw Chad at a softball game. He seemed to be rather dejected, so I asked him, "How are things going?"

"Not very well," he said. "Nina broke up with me last week."

"Why would she do that?" I asked.

"She said it's because I never apologize, and that when I try, I put the blame on her."

"Did she give you any examples?" I inquired.

"Well, the last one—and I guess the one that pushed her over the edge—was that I got angry with her and told her that she was letting her mother come between us. Perhaps I got a little loud. When she complained about my yelling to her, I said, 'I wouldn't be yelling at you if you hadn't put your mother before me.' I didn't see that as blaming her. I was simply telling the truth."

It was obvious to me that Chad had a lot to learn about apologizing. I met with him and Nina for a couple of counseling appointments. I thought he was beginning to gain some insights, but Nina was not willing to continue the relationship. "I can't live with a man who blames me for everything and excuses his own behavior. He hasn't made any efforts to change, although we've talked about this many times. If he can change, that's fine. Then maybe he can have a relationship with someone else. But I can't take any more pain." Chad's failure to apologize led to the death of the relationship.

LOST IN TRANSLATION

The second reason we need to learn and discuss the five languages of an apology is they provide the insight we need in order to apologize effectively. If you are sincerely saying "I'm sorry," but your partner is waiting to hear "I was wrong," then the sincerity of your apology is lost in the translation. To be effective in this case would require speaking the language of "accepting responsibility." Many people believe that they are sincerely apologizing, but their sincerity is not coming through emotionally to the other person.

BEWARE THE RED FLAG

The third reason that understanding apology languages is so important is they give you an indicator of what life will be like if you marry this person. The idea that "love is blind" is never truer than in the area of apology. Sometimes we overlook an offense or excuse the missing apology because of those "in love" feelings. Yet those who are unwilling or lacking understanding in how to give a sincere apology while dating may well bring trouble into the marriage relationship. That's what happened to Jan and Lucas.

At the end of their first year of marriage, Jan was already contemplating her exit strategy. From her perspective, Lucas was caught up in his career and had little time for her. "The worst was the Friday afternoon that he called and said, 'I've gotten tied up at the office. It's going to take me another two or three hours to complete this. I don't want to hold you up, so why don't you just drive up to the cabin and I'll be there later tonight?'"

Jan sat weeping in my office. "This was our anniversary getaway! That's when I realized that I was playing second fiddle to his job."

In my efforts to understand, I probed into the first year of their marriage and found that on numerous occasions Lucas had put his job before his marriage. At least, that was Jan's perspective. "Has he ever apologized for any of these?" I asked.

"No," she said. "He always makes excuses and then the next day sends me roses. I hate his roses. In fact, the last time they came I told the deliveryman to take them to my next-door neighbor and tell her they were from her husband. I figured someone may as well enjoy the roses."

Then I inquired about their dating relationship. They had dated their last two years of college and had married two weeks after graduation. "When you were dating, did you ever feel that his studies interfered with your relationship?"

"Interesting that you would ask that," she said. "It was not so much his studies but his intramural sports events. He was the president of his fraternity, and his big thing was sports. We would sometimes go two weeks and never see each other. He would call and tell me what was going on. At first, it didn't bother me, but later I began to feel that I was second or third on his list of priorities. We argued a lot about it our senior year."

"Did he ever apologize for his behavior?" I asked.

"Come to think of it, he never did. He would always say, 'I'm going to make it up to you when we get married.' I believed him and couldn't wait until we got married. I guess he never changed. He was obsessed with his fraternity, and then after marriage he was obsessed with his job."

Jan's face indicated that the lights had just come on. She later told me that she had never made the connection between his behavior in college and his behavior after they got married.

Lucas grew up in a home where his father never apologized. His father was a very successful businessman, and Lucas intended to follow his example. The problem was he also followed his example in never learning to apologize. Had Jan understood the importance of apologizing in a dating relationship, she would have been able to confront Lucas with this before they got married. Instead, she put up with his excuses and hung her hopes on things being different after marriage.

The ideal scenario would have been for Jan to confront Lucas with the reality that he never apologized; explain to him the necessity of apologizing if relationships are to be healthy; and together learn each other's apology languages, developing a healthy foundation for marriage. Obviously this had not happened.

Fortunately, with counseling, Lucas was able to discover this relational weakness and correct it. As he formulated sincere apologies, he looked more closely at his priorities. He began to break free from his "workaholism," and he and Jan went on to build a solid marriage.

Most people do not radically change behavior patterns after they get married. They simply follow the patterns they have developed before marriage. If they sincerely apologized before marriage, they will do so after marriage. If they did not, then don't expect an apology after marriage.

"It seems so logical," Jan said. "Why didn't I see this when we were dating?"

"Because you were blinded by the 'in love' euphoria," I told her. "Most people do not look at reality when they are 'in love.'"

REMOVING THE RED FLAG

I believe that the single adult who understands the value of apologizing is far more likely to make this an issue for discussion and negotiation while dating. The degree to which the two of them learn to speak each other's apology languages while dating will likely determine the way they deal with offenses after they get married. If there is no progress before marriage, this should be taken as a red flag saying, "It is not time to get married."

Here are three dating couples who made apologizing an issue in their relationship and found that it paid tremendous dividends.

'I Was Ready to Move On'

Sandy was moody and often ruined a beautiful evening by being negative. The soup was too hot, the salad too wilted, and the steak too tough—real encouragement to Ryan who had taken her to a nice restaurant. "At first, I thought it was just that time of the month," he said. "Then I realized it didn't matter which day of the month or where we went; she always found something to complain about. I was ready to mark her off and move on," Ryan said.

"So I told her I thought it was best for us to go our separate ways. She asked me why, so I told her. I figured I had nothing to lose and it might help her."

Then Ryan told me what happened next: "I have never heard such an apology!" he said. "At the time, I didn't know anything about the five apology languages, but she used them all.

"I sensed that she was sincere, so I asked her if she was willing to go see a counselor. She agreed and said she had been thinking about that for some time. The next week she made an appointment. That was the beginning of a real change. In six months, she was like a totally different person.

"That was a year ago, and we are now talking about the possibility of marriage. She is a wonderful person. Now that she has learned to be positive, we are having a great time together."

In Sandy's case, genuine repentance meant seeing a counselor. Some would say that it was counseling that saved their relationship. But the counseling would not have begun without Ryan's loving confrontation, followed by her sincere apology. The apology opened the door for forgiveness, and the counseling allowed growth to take place.

All of us are in process. We all have areas of weakness. When we apologize for our offensive behavior and are willing to take steps to change, we make it possible for our relationships to continue and thrive.

A Fine Fix for the 'Fix-It Man'

Jake and Nikki have been dating for two years. "We got off to a slow start," said Jake. "For the first year, I don't know that either of us would have called it dating. We occasionally had dinner together and played tennis. We both like tennis. Then one night, I had this strong urge to kiss her. I asked her, 'Could I kiss you?' She replied, 'I'm sure you could; would you like to?' 'Yes,' I said and moved toward her lips. I don't know what happened, but from that night on, we were definitely dating.

"Things went well for about six months, and then I began to notice that she was making a lot of comments about my treating her like a child. I didn't know what she was talking about, so I asked her to explain. She said, 'When I share with you a problem from work, you almost always tell me what I should do. The next day you ask me if I did what you told me to do. I don't like that! I feel like you are being my father in both telling me what to do and checking up on me to see if I did it.'

"To be honest with you," Jake said, "her answer blew me away. I was not aware that was the way I was coming across to her. In my mind, I was simply trying to be helpful. I began to read some books and realized that there are a lot of men like me. One book called us *fix-it men*—tell us a problem and we'll give you a solution. I honestly thought that was what she wanted when she shared a problem. Now I understand that what she wanted was empathy, not answers. So, I've learned to say, 'I can see how you could feel upset about that. I probably would feel the same way if I were in your shoes.' I never give her advice unless she asks for it."

"That's right," Nikki said. "He's made a real change. I'll never forget the night he apologized. It was about a week after I confronted him with the problem. I guess it took him awhile to process it all. He began by saying, 'I'm sorry. I didn't realize what I was doing to you. I was honestly trying to be helpful. I realize now that what I did was wrong. It was harmful to our relationship, and I really regret that.' He then asked me what I wanted from him when I shared a problem at work or in some other area of my life. It really impressed me that he was open to change and wanted my input. His apology was so sincere," she said.

"It was a big lesson for me," Jake said. "I had never thought about all of this before. It makes sense to me now, but at the time, I didn't understand anything that was going on. I'm just glad she was willing to give me another chance and not write me off. I feel like our relationship is much closer now that I understand her better. In fact, sometimes she even asks for my advice now. I usually smile and ask, 'Are you really sure you want to hear my advice?' before I give her an answer."

I later discovered that Nikki's primary apology language is genuine repentance and her secondary language is accepting responsibility. When Jake said, "I'm sorry I was wrong. How can I do this differently in the future?" he had definitely spoken her language. Nikki was able to genuinely forgive him because she saw his apology as very sincere.

The Lights Turn On

At the end of a session on the apology languages, Jackson and Sarah came up afterward to say the lights just went on—they realized "a big part of our problem" was that they had not been speaking each other's language.

Jackson would say "I'm sorry," but Sarah needed something else. "What I want to hear him say is 'I was wrong. Will you please forgive me?'" she explained. "Until tonight, I never realized that's what I wanted to hear him say. I just knew that his 'I'm sorry' always seemed inadequate."

I looked at Jackson and asked, "And what is your apology language?"

"Number one is making restitution," he said. "I want her to do something to try to make it up to me."

"And how does she typically apologize?"

"She says, 'I was wrong. Will you please forgive me?' I've always been willing to forgive her, but her apology never quite seemed sincere to me. Now I know why. I always tried to make it up to her by taking her to a nice restaurant or buying her a gift."

"And while I appreciated those things, they never quite took the place of 'I was wrong. Will you please forgive me?'" Sarah said. "In fact, I sometimes saw the gifts and the dinners as an effort to keep from apologizing."

"Thanks for sharing the apology languages," Jackson said. "I think it is going to make a big difference in our relationship."

Eight months later, my wife and I received an invitation to Jackson and Sarah's wedding. I took the occasion to ask, "How are you guys doing in speaking each other's apology languages?"

"We're doing great," Jackson said. "She has learned how to make restitution, and I have learned how to say, 'I was wrong. Will you please forgive me?'"

Sarah added, "And in getting ready for our wedding, we've had lots of opportunities to apologize."

"You are on the road to a good marriage," I said. "Remember, there are no healthy marriages without genuine apologies."

Learning to apologize is a life skill that will make all of your relationships more authentic. Dating should be a time of growth. Few things are more important in a dating relationship than learning each other's primary apology language and learning to speak it fluently.

The FIVE LANGUAGES
of APOLOGY

EXPRESSING REGRET
"I am sorry"

ACCEPTING RESPONSIBILITY
"I was wrong"

MAKING RESTITUTION
"What can I do to make it right?"

GENUINELY REPENTING
"I'll try not to do that again"

REQUESTING FORGIVENESS
"Will you please forgive me?"

13

APOLOGIZING *in the* Workplace

I was at a local bank standing in line, waiting my turn to see a teller. My wait was probably not more than ninety seconds; however, when I arrived before the teller she said with a smile, "I'm sorry you had to wait."

"Not a problem," I said as I handed her my transactions. When she finished she asked, "Is there anything else?"

"That's all," I said.

Then with another smile, she added, "Have a good afternoon."

"Thank you," I responded. "Same to you."

From there I drove to the local post office and stood in line for thirteen minutes. When I arrived at the counter, the postal employee said nothing. "I'd like to send this first class," I said.

Still no comment as she processed the postage. "Three twenty," she said.

I gave her a five; she made the change and handed me my receipt. "Thank you very much," I said as I walked away.

As I drove back to my office, I reflected on those two encounters. My experience at the bank had been pleasant and friendly, while at the post office I felt I was dealing more with a machine rather than a person. *Why did I respond so differently to the two encounters?* I asked myself. Probably because the teller began with an apology for my "wait," while the postal employee made no apology.

Sometime later I thought about the number of times I have walked into that bank and that post office over the past ten years. I realized that each time my reception had been the same. If I waited in line, each teller said, "I'm sorry you had to wait." At the post office, however, I never remember being greeted by any postal employee with those words, though my wait at the post office was always much longer than my wait at the bank.

WHAT SUCCESSFUL COMPANIES KNOW

It seemed apparent to me that the bank employees had been trained to apologize, while the postal employees had not. Consequently, I as a customer much preferred my visits to the bank. Some may argue that the apology of the teller was perfunctory and insincere. And perhaps that is true, but I still appreciated someone acknowledging regret that I had to wait for service.

Successful companies have long understood the power of an apology. Most generally subscribe to the philosophy "The customer is always right." Usually, this means that employees are trained to apologize when a customer complains.

Serving the Customer

Some weeks ago I went to a local pizza restaurant for dinner. Afterward I was talking with the manager of the restaurant. "What do you do when customers get upset or complain about service or food?" I asked. Without hesitation he said, "The customer gets the last word."

"What do you mean by that?" I inquired.

He took a sheet of paper and wrote the following words:

> Listen
> Apologize
> Show concern
> Thank the customer

"That's our policy," he said. "We listen to the customer's complaint. We apologize. We try to show genuine concern for any problem our service has caused them. And we thank them for bringing it to our attention."

"Does that approach seem to work well?" I asked. "So far, so good," he replied. "Fortunately, we don't have too many complaints."

"That's good," I said. "I certainly don't have any complaints. The food was great and the service superb."

"Thanks," he said. "That's our goal."

I continued, "I've been doing some research on apologies over the past two years. Would you like to know what I've learned?" "Certainly," he said.

Since he had written out his plan for handling upset customers, I decided to write the five apology languages. So I listed them as follows:

> Expressing regret—"I am sorry."
> Accepting responsibility—"I was wrong."
> Making restitution—"What can I do to make it right?"
> Genuinely repenting—"I'll try not to do that again."
> Requesting forgiveness—"Will you please forgive me?"

I explained that our research had indicated that each person has a primary apology language, and if you don't speak their language, they may consider your apology to be weak and unacceptable; that's why sometimes even though you apologize, a customer may continue to be irate and will likely not return to your establishment. "Have you ever had this experience?" I asked.

A Restaurant Spill

"As a matter of fact, about three weeks ago two ladies came in for dinner. Our waitress accidentally spilled a soda on one of the ladies. She apologized immediately and got paper towels and cleaned up the table and invited the ladies to move to another table. The waitress told me what had happened, so I walked out and asked the ladies if everything was all right."

"Not really," she said. "In fact, I've got to go home and change clothes before I can continue my evening. This is not what I had in mind when I came in here to eat."

"I could tell that she was still pretty hot," he said, "so I tried our last approach."

"What actually happened?" I asked.

"I listened as she explained how the waitress had spilled the drink on her blouse and skirt, how cold and now how stained and sticky she felt. I said to her, 'I'm really sorry that happened. That is certainly not what we want for our customers. Let me assure you that I will be happy to pay the cleaning bill for your clothes, and this meal is on the house. We appreciate your business, and we certainly don't want this kind of thing to happen.'

"Her response was 'Well, it didn't have to happen if she hadn't been in such a hurry.'

"'I'll be happy to assign you another waitress,' I said as I walked away. I did, but as the lady walked out of the door, she was talking about how awful she looked and felt and that if she had known this would happen, she would not have come in the first place. It was embarrassing for me that other customers heard her comment, but I didn't know what else to do."

"Let's see which of the five apology languages you spoke," I said. I checked off number one as I said, "You definitely expressed regret when you said, 'I'm really sorry that happened.' I'm not sure you or the waitress accepted responsibility. I didn't hear either of you saying, 'I was wrong. It was my fault.' You did, however, make restitution by offering to pay the cleaning bill and giving her the meal free. I didn't hear any genuine repentance; that is, you expressed no plan for seeing that this didn't happen in the future. Nor did you ask her to forgive you. So it seems to me that you spoke two of the five apology languages."

"Apparently, her language was one of the other three," I continued. "Perhaps if you had spoken her language, she may have accepted your apology and even expressed forgiveness."

"That's an interesting idea," he said. "I'll have to think about that."

Six weeks later, I stopped by for another pizza. The manager came over and sat down. He said, "I've taught all my employees the five languages of an apology. The next time we have a problem, we're ready. We are going to speak all five apology languages."

"Good," I said. "Then you are bound to hit the person's primary apology language. I predict you will see a difference in the way the person responds."

The Pizza Man Delivers . . . at Home

The manager continued, "This also works in a marriage, doesn't it?"

"Why do you say that?" I asked.

"Because I've discovered that my wife's apology language is genuine repentance. She wants me to assure her that I have a plan so that this won't happen again. In the past, I've been big on 'I'm sorry.' That has never been very effective with her. When I shared the five apology languages with her, she immediately said, 'That's the whole problem with your apologies. They always end with "I'm sorry."'"

"And what is your apology language?" I asked.

"Accepting responsibility," he said. "I want her to say 'I was wrong.' In the past, she has seldom said those words, which always made me feel that her apologies were not sincere."

"This works in all human relationships," I said. "I predict that your business and your marriage will both improve. Do you want my counseling bill now, or do you want me to mail it to you?" I joked.

As our conversation was ending, I quietly added, "And one other thing—don't forget to apologize to your employees when you lose your temper and speak harshly to them."

"How did you know that?" he asked.

I smiled and said, "I just assumed that you are human."

"I've got an employee I need to apologize to right now," he said.

"Do you know her apology language?" I asked.

"Not really," he said. "So I'm going to use all five."

THE *LEARN* POLICY

During the past two years, I have asked numerous employees this question: Does your company have a policy on how to deal with irate customers? Almost without exception, the answer has been yes. For some the policy is vague but involves some attempt to listen to the customer's complaint and make some effort to respond in a positive way. For others, their policy has been stated in clear and specific terms.

Wise companies have consistent and specific plans for their employees to follow to "make things right." Recently I was spending the night in a Dallas hotel. I asked the young man who was running the front desk my question: Does the hotel have a policy on how to respond to irate customers? I assured him I was not angry, but I was doing research on customers who are upset.

His response was very clear. "Our plan is based on the acrostic LEARN." He then announced them clearly.

L = Listen. Hear the customer's complaint.

E = Empathize. Let the customer know that you understand why they would be upset.

A = Apologize.

R = Respond and react. Try to make things right.

N = Notify. Get back in touch with the customer and let them know what action has been taken.[1]

Clearly this employee was well trained!

WHEN DOCTORS APOLOGIZE

Research indicates that many professions are becoming more apology conscious in recent years—among them the medical profession. In the past, medical doctors have been looked upon as godlike, their decisions seldom questioned. Today, more and more doctors are seeing the value of apologizing to patients when they make mistakes in judgment or action. This movement to apologize has been prompted, in part, by emerging evidence about the scope of medical errors. The Institute of Medicine report in 1999 said, "Mistakes kill as many as 98,000 hospitalized Americans each year."[2]

Fewer Lawsuits

Consequently, the hospitals in the University of Michigan Health System have been encouraging doctors since 2002 to apologize for mistakes. The system's annual attorney fees have since dropped from three million to one million dollars, and malpractice lawsuits and notices of intent to sue have fallen from 262 filed in 2001 to about 130 per year, according to Rick Boothman, a former trial attorney who launched the practice there.[3]

Patients have responded extremely positively to such apologies. Linda Kenney, a mother of three, almost died seven years ago when anesthesia was improperly administered prior to her surgery. "My husband wanted to sue," she told a reporter. "He really wanted some-one to pay." But then the anesthesiologist wrote her a letter express-ing his grief and contrition. Dr. Rick van Pelt wrote, "Whenever you want to speak, I'll make myself available. Here's my home number and my beeper number."

At first she thought he was just trying to cover himself. But no: "Rick stuck his neck out. He met me in my hometown. . . . He made himself totally vulnerable to me. He not only apologized but also acknowledged how emotional the event had been for him, for his family, and for me."[4]

Linda Kenney saw the apology as genuine, and she later dropped her plan for litigation. Subsequently Dr. van Pelt joined her to found an organization that helps those involved with medical and surgical errors to deal with the aftermath.[5]

'He Just Didn't Care'

Colorado surgeon Michael Woods was overseeing surgery to remove a patient's appendix when a medical student accidentally punctured an artery. Although the appendix was successfully removed, the oper-ation became complicated. The patient was unhappy with how Woods handled the aftermath and sued him for malpractice. Woods took the traditional approach recommended by his attorney—no response and no interaction between him and the patient.

In the courtroom, when the patient was asked why she had cho-sen to sue, she said, "I sued because he acted like what happened to me was no big deal. He just didn't care."

Later Dr. Woods said, "That comment hit me like the heat from a blast furnace. It wasn't the injury and outcome that had led to that miserable day in court—it was her perception that I didn't care. My actions had communicated apathy and that was what had landed me in court, not the medical complication."[6] Woods realized that his failure to offer a sincere apology was probably the reason she had filed suit.

In his revealing book *Healing Words: The Power of Apology in Medicine*, Dr. Woods adds: "The business world has internalized a truth that medicine has yet to discover and embrace: Apology isn't about money or being right or wrong—for either the buyer (patient) or the vendor (doctor). It's about the provider showing respect, empathy, and a commitment to patient satisfaction; and about those receiving the apology having the grace to see the provider as human and fallible—and worthy of forgiveness."[7]

When doctors have chosen to apologize for their mistakes, the results have been extremely gratifying, so gratifying, in fact, that one insurance company has now taken a pro-apology stance with the medical doctors it insures.[8]

THE NEED TO APOLOGIZE TO OUR COWORKERS

While many companies and professions have seen the value of apologizing to customers and clients, we have discovered that few companies have made any effort to train their employees on the value of apologizing to each other. And we did not discover a single company that had, as a part of their training program, any emphasis on how to apologize effectively to fellow employees.

As adults, many of us spend the largest amount of our hours each day in our place of employment. The standard in North America is eight hours per day, but many people spend ten hours or even more. When we subtract the time we spend sleeping, we realize that we spend more time with the people with whom we work than we do our families.

With our work associates we have a relationship. It may be casual or close, depending on the nature of our jobs and the choices we make. In work relationships, there is the potential for fostering appreciation and encouragement. There is also the potential for offense, hurt feelings, anger, and tension. Most of us prefer to work in an environment that is friendly, supportive, and positive. However, most of us have sometimes found ourselves at odds with a coworker. During such occasions, understanding the value of apologizing becomes extremely important.

While interest in apologizing in the workplace is increasing, there is a realization that apologizing is not as easy as it sounds. Most people have only a limited idea of what it means to apologize. "I apologize." "I'm sorry." "I was wrong." "I'm sorry I hurt you." "I'm sorry you were hurt by what I said." All of these are considered apologies by different individuals.

A Great Workplace Project

If you're a workplace supervisor or manager, here's how you can help: Ask your staff to share with one another their primary apology language. Then all of you will know how to more effectively apologize to one another. What a great workplace project! That's what I told the pizza manager to do the night he was about to apologize to an employee—sometime in the future have the staff tell each other their primary apology language. He spoke all five languages that night, so he probably was successful. But knowing their apology language would make future apologies most effective.

Our suggestion is that employers expose their employees to the concept of the five languages of apology; then help them discover their own primary apology language. Finally, have them reveal this information to the circle of employees with whom they interact.

What many coworkers do not realize is that people have different apology languages, and if they don't speak their colleagues' specific language, the coworkers will not hear the apology as being sincere. By learning to apologize more effectively, we can have better relationships with our coworkers. That can make for a happier, more pleasant workplace.

The Receptionist's Apology

Recently a colleague whom I'll call Dr. Mary told me (Jennifer) about a particular receptionist who worked in her counseling office years ago. The receptionist at times forgot to remove a client's name from the appointment book after the person called to cancel a session. Dr. Mary would come to the office, and the client would not show up.

She would say to the receptionist, "I'm concerned about this person." The receptionist would answer, "Oh, I just remembered that she cancelled last week and I forgot to mark that down."

Of course, Dr. Mary would have a wasted hour. The first time this happened, she just accepted the receptionist's apology and moved on. The next time it happened, the receptionist was again very apologetic. "I'm sorry," she said. "I just forgot."

Dr. Mary wanted to be gracious and offer forgiveness a second time. However, the words got stuck in her throat. There was a tension between the two. The apology seemed incomplete and insincere to Dr. Mary, and she was concerned that her receptionist really had not changed.

So she said to the receptionist, "I really would hate to be in this same place again next week, because it is uncomfortable for both of us, and it carries real cost for me. So can we talk about what you can do differently to be sure that you get clients erased when they cancel and inform me as quickly as possible? I think we could work together more comfortably this way."

The receptionist agreed, and after some discussion they both decided that the receptionist would keep a legal pad on her desk. At the top of the front page was the word *Cancellations*. She agreed that immediately upon receiving a cancellation, she would write the client's name and the name of the counselor whom the client was to see. And on the second line, she would write the words *Informed the counselor* and record the date and time that she actually informed the counselor of the cancellation.

With this plan of genuine repentance, Dr. Mary was able to accept the receptionist's apology and go on with her workday. Her primary apology language was genuine repentance. She was willing to accept a simple "I'm sorry" the first time but not the second time. Had she not requested a plan for making things different in the future and had the receptionist not complied with that plan, their relationship would have been estranged.

Apologies = Good Business

Jennifer's illustration affirms two essentials in building healthy relationships. One, we must let coworkers know what we expect in an apology. And second, the offender must be willing to speak the apology language of the one who was offended. When these two essentials are in place, we can create a positive emotional environment in which to work. That's why Jennifer and I recommend coworkers read this book, discover their own primary apology language, and tell their coworkers during a staff meeting. We believe that these simple steps would create a much more wholesome and healthy work environment for thousands of employees.

Creating a positive emotional work environment enhances the productivity of employees. Thus, a company that has the vision not only of apologizing to customers and clients but teaching employees how to apologize effectively to one another is the company that is more likely to succeed in accomplishing its financial objectives. Bottom line: Learning to apologize is good business. The employees live with less stress and anxiety, while the company profits from their increased productivity.

The FIVE LANGUAGES
of APOLOGY

EXPRESSING REGRET
"I am sorry"

ACCEPTING RESPONSIBILITY
"I was wrong"

MAKING RESTITUTION
"What can I do to make it right?"

GENUINELY REPENTING
"I'll try not to do that again"

REQUESTING FORGIVENESS
"Will you please forgive me?"

CHAPTER

14

APOLOGIZING *to* Yourself

Jordan was in my office crying—*sobbing* would be a better word. I have known him for all of his eighteen years, but I had never seen him this emotionally disturbed. He had always seemed so self-assured. He was a good student, a star football player, and had been active in the church youth program. In short, he was the all-American model teenager. However, in my office, none of that seemed to matter. He spoke slowly at first, trying to hold back the tears.

"I've really blown it," he said. "I've messed up my whole life. I really wish I could die." With those three statements, I knew that Jordan was in serious trouble.

"Would you like to tell me about it?" I asked. Jordan looked at the floor as he talked.

"It all started last year," he said. "I met this girl at school. I knew I should not have dated her, but she was so good-looking. I started taking her home after school. I found out her father had left four years ago and her mother didn't get home from work until about 6 p.m. We would study together and talk. Then we started messing around, and before long, we were having sex. I knew it wasn't right, but I tried to be careful. She got pregnant anyway, and last week she had an abortion."

Jordan's whole body was shaking. Tears were falling on his jeans like rain. A full minute later, he said, "I let my parents down. I let God down. I let myself down. I let her down. I just wish I could die."

Jordan was young, but he was wise enough to know that he needed help. For the next twelve months, I saw him regularly. I watched him step up to the plate and apologize to his parents, the young woman, and her mother. I saw him weep as he acknowledged to God that he had sinned and asked for His forgiveness. Near the end of our year of counseling (he was now a freshman in college), Jordan said to me, "I think there is one more apology I need to make."

"What's that?" I asked.

"I think I need to apologize to myself."

"That's interesting. Why would you say that?"

"I keep beating myself up," he said. "I keep remembering what I did and feeling bad about it. I don't think I have ever forgiven myself. Everybody else seems to have forgiven me—but *I* haven't forgiven me. Maybe if I could apologize to myself, I could forgive myself."

"I think you're dead right," I said. "Why don't we work on an apology? What would you like to say to yourself?"

Jordan started talking and I started writing. "I'd like to tell myself that I did wrong; I mean really wrong, grossly wrong. I'd like to tell myself how bad I feel about it and how much I regret what I did. I'd like to tell myself that I have learned my lesson, and I will keep myself sexually pure from now until the day I get married. I'd like to give myself the freedom to be happy again. And I'd like to ask myself to forgive me and to help me make the most of my life in the future."

I had been writing furiously to capture Jordan's words. "Give me just a moment," I said. I turned to my computer and typed in Jordan's apology, inserting his name. I printed off a copy and turned to him and said, "I want you to stand in front of this mirror and give your apology to yourself." I listened and watched as Jordan read his apology. Here is what Jordan said:

"Jordan, I want to tell you that I did wrong; I mean really wrong, grossly wrong. Jordan, I want to tell you how bad I feel about it and how much I regret what I did. I want to tell you that I have learned my lesson, and I will keep myself sexually pure from now until the day I get married. I want to give myself the freedom to be happy again. And, Jordan, I want to ask you to forgive me and to help me make the most of my life in the future."

Then Jordan turned to me, and I said, "Go ahead, read the last sentence." He continued, *"Jordan, because I believe your apology is sincere, I choose to forgive you."*

The tears were flowing freely down his face as he turned and we embraced. For a full minute we both wept in the thrill of forgiveness. Jordan went on to finish college and is now married, with his own family. He said to me several years after our counseling experience, "The most significant part of my journey was the day I apologized and forgave myself. I don't think I would have made it if that had not happened."

As a counselor, I learned from Jordan firsthand the tremendous power of apologizing to oneself.

WHO WE ARE—WHO WE WANT TO BE

Why would you apologize to yourself? In a general sense, you apologize to yourself for the same reason you apologize to someone else: You want to restore the relationship. When you apologize to someone else, you hope the apology will remove the barrier between the two of you so that your relationship can continue to grow. When you apologize to yourself, you are seeking to remove the emotional disequilibrium between the person you *want* to be (the ideal self) and the person you *are* (the real self). The greater the distance between the ideal self and the real self, the greater the intensity of the inner emotional turmoil. Being "at peace with oneself" occurs when we remove the distance between the ideal self and the real self. Apologizing to oneself—and subsequently experiencing forgiveness—serves to remove the distance.

Our Moral Failures

Sometimes the emotional anxiety stems from perceived failure to live up to one's moral standards. This was the case with Jordan. He had promised himself that he would never become sexually active before marriage. He knew this was not a moral standard accepted by all teenagers, but for him it was a spiritual issue. He believed that this was God's standard, and he intended to follow it. When he consciously violated his internalized moral standards, he was assailed by anxiety and guilt. For him, the distance between the ideal self and the real self was immense. His apologies to others had served to heal relationships, but until he apologized to himself he did not find inner peace.

Moral failures occur on many fronts. Neal was a forty-five-year-old father of two. He had taught his boys from an early age to tell the truth. Integrity was a high moral value for him, and he wanted his boys to learn to tell the truth. One year as he was filling out his federal tax return, he "stretched the truth" in order to get a larger deduction. At the time, it seemed like a little thing and inconsequential. But within a week, Neal was experiencing strong misgivings about what he had done. It was not until he filed an amended tax return and apologized and forgave himself that he returned to a state of emotional equilibrium.

Lying, stealing, cheating, and sexual immorality are all examples of broken moral standards that can lead to guilt and anxiety. While apologizing to others may bring healing to human relationships, self-apology and forgiveness remove the anxiety and restore peace of mind.

'I Can't Believe I Did That'

When we feel we've behaved badly, our view of ourselves is damaged, even though our bad behavior might not be immoral or even very significant. We thought we were "more mature"—and we beat ourselves up.

Ellen from New England said to me, "I can't believe I was so immature. I created a scene over a discrepancy in a meal charge. I treated the waiter harshly and drew attention to myself from people at other tables. I have been reliving that scene for weeks now. I used to think I was a pretty decent person . . . but now I don't know."

Ellen is suffering with severely damaged self-esteem. The difference between her ideal self and real self are causing her great emotional pain. Ellen needs to apologize to herself.

From Anxiety to Depression?

Another reason for apologizing to yourself is that you may fear the consequences if you continue to hold this offense against yourself. You have lived with emotional anxiety since the offense occurred, and you fear that you are slipping into depression. It is at this point that some people turn to medication to treat the feelings of depression rather than dealing with the event that stimulated these feelings. Medication can be extremely helpful for people who have been depressed for long periods of time or are depressed due to a chemical imbalance in the brain—clinically depressed. However, much depression could be avoided if people would learn to apologize to others and then to themselves.

Moving Past the Failure and Toward the Future

Another reason for apologizing to yourself is to enable you to get back on track in reaching the goals you have established in life. Davis is an aspiring businessman who made an unwise response to another businessman in town. He said to me, "I feel like I have shot myself in the foot. I apologized to the person involved, and I think he has forgiven me. But I am afraid that what I did is going to affect my business for a long time to come. I'm having a hard time shaking it and getting motivated to go on. I've even thought about moving to another city and starting over." Davis is struggling with intense anxiety over the matter, and it is affecting the way he operates his business. He needs to apologize to himself so he can focus on the future and not on past failures.

When you are plagued with anxiety over a past failure, the answer is not "trying to forget it." The more you try to forget it, the bigger it becomes in your mind. The answer lies in apologizing to the offended parties and then apologizing and forgiving yourself.

Unfortunately, it is the disparity between the ideal and the real self that leads many people to alcohol and drugs. It is an unconscious attempt to relieve anxiety. The reality is that such attempts never make things better. Typically when people are under the influence of alcohol or drugs, they make further unwise decisions that create additional anxiety. If they continue to follow this pattern, they may well become addicted to alcohol or drugs, which becomes a problem in and of itself and creates another whole set of problems that produce further anxiety.

WAYS TO DEAL WITH SELF-ANGER

When we fail to live up to our ideal self, what happens inside of us is what happens inside others when we offend them: We become angry. This anger is turned toward self. Ignoring self-anger does not solve the problem. Anger needs to be processed in a positive way.

The Wrong Way: Explosion and Implosion

Two negative ways to process self-anger are explosion and implosion. When we explode with anger, we create further hurt and anger in other people, thus damaging our relationships. When we implode, we express our anger toward ourselves. This may take the form of berating yourself mentally. *I'm stupid; I'm dumb; I'll never get it right; I'll never amount to anything.* These are the attitudes of implosive anger. An extreme case of implosion may express itself by physically abusing one's body. Wrist cutting, head banging, and hair pulling are examples of personal physical abuse. Self-anger expressed by explosion or implosion never improves a situation.

The Right Way

The positive way to process anger involves three steps. First, admit to yourself that what you did was unwise, wrong, or hurtful to others and to yourself. Second, apologize to the people you have offended, and hope they will forgive you. Third, consciously apologize to yourself and choose to forgive yourself.

HOW DO I APOLOGIZE TO MYSELF?

Apologizing to oneself requires *self-talk*. Perhaps you have heard someone say, "Talking to yourself is a sign of mental illness." Wrong! Mentally healthy people always talk to themselves—encouraging themselves, advising themselves, questioning themselves. Some of this self-talk is done aloud; much of it is done mentally and silently. When it comes to apologizing to yourself, I like to encourage audible self-talk. If you are aware of your own primary apology language, then focus on speaking that language, but include the other four languages for additional emotional credit.

At the time I counseled with Jordan, I had not discovered the five languages of an apology. However, in retrospect Jordan did an excellent job of speaking all five languages to himself. My guess is that

Jordan's primary apology language was accepting responsibility. I say that because he began his self-apology by saying, "I did wrong; really and grossly wrong. I really regret what I did." I have discovered that when people offer an apology, many times they will begin by expressing it in their own apology language. They are saying to others what they would expect others to say to them if they were apologizing.

So begin with the apology language that seems best for you. Then seek to include the other four languages.

We suggest that you write out your self-apology before you speak it to yourself. Here is a summary of the apology that Jordan made to himself. We have removed his name and left the blanks so you can include your name. You may change the order of his statements, and you may change the wording. We offer it simply to help you get started in forming your self-apology.

"_____, I want to tell you that I did wrong; I mean really wrong, grossly wrong. _____, I want to tell you how bad I feel about it and how much I regret what I did. I want to tell you that I have learned my lesson. _____, I want to give myself the freedom to be happy again. And, _____, I want to ask you to forgive me and to help me make the most of my life in the future. _____, because I believe your apology is sincere, I choose to forgive you."

Go ahead and write your self-apology statement. After you have written that self-apology, we encourage you to stand in front of the mirror, look yourself in the eyes, and audibly give your apology to yourself. We believe that apologizing to yourself is an important step in the process of restoring "peace with yourself."

WHAT DOES IT MEAN TO FORGIVE MYSELF?

Forgiving oneself is much like forgiving someone who has offended you. Forgiving someone else means that you choose to no longer hold the offense against them. You will accept them back into your life and will seek to continue building your relationship with them. Their offense is no longer a barrier in your relationship. If a wall is seen as a symbol of their offense against you, forgiveness tears down the wall. Forgiveness allows the two of you to communicate again and to listen to each other with a view to understanding. It opens up the potential of working together as a team.

The same is true in forgiving oneself. At its root, self-forgiveness is a choice. We feel pained at our wrongdoing. We wish we had not committed the offense. The reality is that we have. We have apologized to other parties who were involved if our offense was against others. Perhaps we have asked God's forgiveness. We have also apologized to ourselves. Now it is time to forgive ourselves. We must choose to do so. No positive purpose is served by berating ourselves explosively or implosively. All such behavior is destructive. Choosing to forgive oneself removes the distance between the ideal self and the real self. In forgiving ourselves, we are affirming our high ideals. We are admitting our failures and affirming our commitment to our ideals.

As you wrote your self-apology statement, we also encourage you to write your self-forgiveness statement. Here is a sample that may stimulate your own thinking.

"_____, the offense you committed has troubled me greatly. It has brought me much inner anxiety. But I have heard your sincere apology and I value you. Therefore, _____, I choose to forgive you. I will no longer hold the offense against you. I will do everything I can to make your future bright. You can count on my support. Let me say it again, _____: I forgive you."

After you have written your forgiveness statement, again we urge you to stand in front of the mirror, look yourself in the eyes, and audibly express your forgiveness.

As in forgiving others, this self-forgiveness does not remove all the pain or memories of your failure, nor does it necessarily remove all the results of your failure. For example, if you have lied or stolen, you may still face the results of those actions. What forgiveness does is to release you from the bondage of your past failures and give you the freedom to make the most of the future.

LEARNING FROM YOUR FAILURES

You are now in a position to change the course of your life. Sometimes people make the mistake of trying never to think again about the failure. The fact is we can learn much from our failures. Ask yourself, *What are the factors that led me to the offense?* Those are things that need to be changed.

For example, if you fell into the abuse of alcohol or drugs, it may be that you put yourself into a situation that fostered drinking or drug use. In the future, you must not allow this to happen. If your failure was sexual immorality, then you must remove yourself from the environment that would encourage you to repeat that failure.

In addition to learning from past failures, you are now in a position to take positive steps to make your future brighter. This may involve reading books, attending seminars, talking with friends, or counseling. These are the kinds of steps that give you new information and insights with which to direct your future. Apologizing to yourself and choosing to forgive yourself opens to you the possibility of a future that is far brighter than you have ever dreamed.

The FIVE LANGUAGES
of APOLOGY

EXPRESSING REGRET
"I am sorry"

ACCEPTING RESPONSIBILITY
"I was wrong"

MAKING RESTITUTION
"What can I do to make it right?"

GENUINELY REPENTING
"I'll try not to do that again"

REQUESTING FORGIVENESS
"Will you please forgive me?"

15

What If We All **LEARNED** *to* **Apologize** *Effectively?*

When our granddaughter Davy Grace was five years old, her mother and father allowed her to spend a special week with her grandparents. Karolyn and I were elated. The week was great fun. But one experience is indelibly printed in my memory. Karolyn has a special drawer where she keeps "stickers" for the grandchildren. Davy Grace, of course, knew about this special drawer and asked her grandmother if she could have some stickers. Karolyn told her that she could have three, any three she chose.

An hour or two later, we began to see stickers all over the house. Davy Grace had taken the entire sheet of stickers and placed them randomly. Karolyn said to her, "I thought I told you to take only three stickers, but you have taken the whole sheet."

Davy Grace stood in silence as her grandmother continued. "You disobeyed Grandmother."

Tears cascaded down Davy Grace's face as she said, "I need somebody to forgive me."

I shall never forget those words nor the pain that I saw in her young face. My tears joined her tears as I embraced her and said, "Honey, all of us need somebody to forgive us. And Papa will be happy to forgive you, and I'm sure Grandmother will also." Karolyn joined us in our hug of reconciliation.

SOMEBODY TO FORGIVE US

I have reflected upon that scene many times while I have been writing this book on apology. I'm convinced that the need for forgiveness is universal and that acknowledging that need is the essence of an apology.

Apologies grow out of an awareness that my words or behavior has violated the trust of others or has offended them in some way. When these offenses go unacknowledged, the relationship is fractured. I live with a sense of guilt or a smug self-righteousness while the offended party lives with hurt, disappointment, and/or anger. We both know that our relationship has suffered from the offense. If neither of us extends the olive branch, the quality of our relationship will continue to diminish.

Several years ago while living in Chicago, I often volunteered at the Pacific Garden Mission. I met scores of men and a few women who shared with me their journey to the streets. I recognized a common thread through all of their stories. All of them had a series of experiences in which someone treated them unfairly. (At least this was their perception.) And no one ever apologized. Many of them admitted that they also had treated others unkindly and failed to apologize. A string of broken relationships was the result. Eventually, there was no one to whom they could turn, so they turned to the streets. I have often wondered how different things might have been had someone taught these men and women to apologize by apologizing.

On the other end of the social spectrum is corporate America. In recent years, we have seen numerous corporate executives indicted and sometimes convicted of fraud. One wonders what would have happened if these executives had learned to apologize when they were climbing up the corporate ladder.

Many government employees have also joined the ranks of the convicted. Most of them have pleaded innocent until they were proven guilty. When apologies have been made, they tended to be stated in very nebulous terms and often appeared self-serving. In the case of government and public executives, the reluctance to apologize may grow out of fear that the apology will be used against them. They reason, *Better to keep quiet and maintain my position than to apologize and lose everything.* Many have never come to understand that there are things in life more important than power and money. Albert Einstein once wrote, "Sometimes what counts can't be counted, and what can be counted doesn't count."[1]

BREAKING THE PATTERNS OF OUR CULTURE

For the "ordinary" man or woman, the reluctance to apologize is rooted in cultural patterns that they observed and internalized while growing up. Thus, as we have discussed earlier, some jump immediately into the blame mode, blaming others for their failures. Others, with a stone face, deny that any offense has been committed. Still others make a quick and weak apology, hoping to put the matter behind them.

However, a growing number of people are learning to slow down and take time to genuinely apologize. These are the strong ones; these are the heroes; these are the ones whom people like to be around; these are the ones whom people trust.

IF APOLOGIES WERE A WAY OF LIFE

The art of apologizing is not easy, but it can be learned, and it is worth the effort. Apologizing opens up a whole new world of emotional and spiritual health. Having apologized, we are able to look ourselves in the mirror, look people in the eyes, and worship God "in spirit and in truth." It is those who truly apologize who are most likely to be truly forgiven.

If apologizing were a way of life, no walls would be built. Relationships would be authentic. Certainly people would fail, but the failures would be dealt with in an open and honest manner. Regret would be expressed; responsibility would be accepted. Restitution would be made. Genuine repentance would be our intention, and we would stand humbly and say, "I need somebody to forgive me." I believe in most cases if we learned to apologize effectively, we would be genuinely forgiven.

When apology becomes a way of life, relationships will remain healthy. People will find the acceptance, support, and encouragement they need. Fewer people would turn to drugs and alcohol in an effort to find escape from broken relationships. And fewer people would live on the streets of America.

Yes, Davy Grace, I too need somebody to forgive me. From five to eighty-five, we all need someone to forgive us. That is more likely to happen if we learn to apologize effectively. May this book move all of us into the apology mode. May we learn to recognize and overcome our tendency to blame, deny, or offer quick and weak apologies without truly dealing with the offense.

As we close this book, perhaps you would like to join us in this prayer: "Father, give me the attitude of Davy Grace: 'I need somebody to forgive me,' and teach me how to apologize effectively. Amen."

Notes

Chapter 1: Why Apologize?

1. Gary D. Chapman, *The Five Love Languages of Teenagers* (Chicago: Northfield, 2000).

2. Matthew 6:15 NKJV.

3. Ephesians 4:32; 1 John 1:9.

4. Luke 23:34.

5. Acts 2:22–24, 40–41.

6. Romans 12:19.

7. For a further explanation of how to release stored anger, see Gary Chapman, *The Other Side of Love: Handling Anger in a Godly Way* (Chicago: Moody, 1999).

8. Dietrich Bonhoeffer, *The Cost of Discipleship* (New York: Macmillan, 1963), 47.

Chapter 2: Apology Language # 1: Expressing Regret

1. Robert Fulghum, *All I Really Need to Know I Learned in Kindergarten* (New York: Ballantine, 1986), 4.

Chapter 3: Apology Language # 2: Accepting Responsibility

1. As quoted in Ken Blanchard and Margret McBride, *The One Minute Apology* (New York: Harper Collins, 2003), 1.

2. Ibid., x.

3. Patrick T. Reardon, "Oprah Turns on Memoir Author," *Chicago Tribune*, 27 January 2006, sec. 1.

4. See Charlie Madigan, "A Million Little Pieces," *Chicago Tribune*, 26 January 2006, www.chicagotribune. com/news/nationworld/chi-gleaner,1,3854195.hltml?coll=chi-newscolumnists-utl; and Steve Johnson, "All Praise Oprah," *Chicago Tribune*, 26 January 2006, http://featuresblogs.chicagotribune. com/technology_internetcritic/2006/01.

5. Reardon, "Oprah Turns on Memoir Author," *Chicago Tribune*.

6. Ephesians 5:25–33.

7. Romans 3:23.

8. 1 John 1:8–10.

Chapter 4: Apology Language # 3: Making Restitution

1. Andy Stanley, *Since Nobody's Perfect . . . How Good Is Good Enough?* (Sisters, Oreg.: Multnomah, 2003), 72.

2. Everett L. Worthington Jr., *Forgiving and Reconciling* (Downers Grove, Ill.: InterVarsity, 2003), 205.

3. For an in-depth look at expressing the five love languages among adults, see my books *The Five Love Languages* (Chicago: Moody, 1992) and *The Five Love Languages for Singles* (Chicago: Northfield, 2003).

4. See Luke 19:1–10.

Chapter 5: Apology Language # 4: Genuinely Repenting

1. "How It Works," *Alcoholics Anonymous* (New York: Alcoholics Anonymous World Services, Inc., 1976), 59.

2. "Armstrong, Lance," *Microsoft Encarta Online Encyclopedia 2005,* http://encarta.msn.com.

Chapter 6: Apology Language # 5: Requesting Forgiveness

1. We conducted a survey of more than 370 adults during 2004–2005 at various marriage seminars, and also collected responses on the Web site garychapman.com. This was a nonscientific survey but included married and single respondents. Most of the respondents at the seminars were married or engaged couples. The survey/questionnaire included seven questions.

2. Remember, for those with a controlling personality, asking forgiveness is out of their comfort zone emotionally. To successfully learn to speak the apology language of requesting forgiveness or, for that matter, any of the apology languages, an extremely controlling individual will likely require the help of an outside party: God, a counselor, a pastor, or a friend who is willing to be honest with him or her.

3. Joanne Kaufman, "Forgive Me!" *Good Housekeeping*, November 2004, 174.

Chapter 8: Apologizing Is a Choice

1. Romans 12:17–19 NKJV.

Chapter 9: Learning to Forgive

1. Robert Enright, http://www.forgiveness-Institute.org/html/about_forgivenss.htm.

2. Psalm 103:12.

3. Psalm 103:10.

4. Isaiah 43:25.

5. Isaiah 59:2.

6. Romans 6:23.

7. Ibid.

8. See Acts 2:37–39.

9. 1 John 1:9.

10. See Ephesians 4:32.

11. Matthew 7:12.

12. See Matthew 5:23–24. Those who want to worship God first should take care of any sin against someone else, seeking reconciliation with the person, Jesus said.

13. 1 Corinthians 11:31–32.

14. Luke 17:3–4 NKJV.

15. Matthew 18:15–16 NKJV.

16. Romans 12:19.

17. 1 Peter 2:23.

18. 1 Peter 2:23, Richard Francis Weymouth, *The New Testament in Modern Speech* (London: Clarue and Company, 2001).

Chapter 10: Learning to Apologize in the Family

1. See Luke 15:11–16.

2. See Luke 15:17–24.

Chapter 11: Teaching Your Child to Apologize

1. Robert Fulghum, *All I Really Need to Know I Learned in Kindergarten* (New York: Ballantine, 1986), 4.

2. The Golden Rule is a rule of conduct toward others given by Jesus: "Do to others as you would have them do to you" (Luke 6:31).

Chapter 12: Apologizing in Dating Relationships

1. Gary Chapman, *The Five Love Languages for Singles* (Chicago: Northfield, 2004), 169–74, 182–92.

Chapter 13: Apologizing in the Workplace

1. The L.E.A.R.N. acronym was originally developed by Debra J. Schmidt and is published in special report #8, "How to Turn Angry Customers into Loyal Customers." It may be purchased at http://theloyaltyleader.com/special_reports.iml. Debra leads businesses to greater customer, employee, and brand loyalty. For more information, visit www.theloyaltyleader.com.

2. *Greensboro (North Carolina) News & Record*, 12 November 2004, A6.

3. Ibid.

4. Joanne Kaufman, "Forgive Me!" *Good Housekeeping*, November 2004, 173–74.

5. Ibid. Their organization is Medical Induced Trauma Support Services.

6. Michael S. Woods, *Healing Words: The Power of Apology in Medicine* (Oak Park, Ill.: Doctors in Touch, 2004), 9.

7. Ibid., 17.

8. Ibid., 61–62.

Chapter 15: What If We All Learned to Apologize Effectively?

1. Michael S. Woods, *Healing Words* (Oak Park, Ill.: Doctors in Touch, 2004), 19.

The FIVE LANGUAGES of APOLOGY

By Dillon Burroughs

HOW TO USE THIS GUIDE

This 14-session Group Study Guide for *The Five Languages of Apology* is intended to maximize your personal learning efforts through small group dialogue and encouragement. Helpful for small groups, workplace studies, book club reading groups, or even shared with a spouse or close friend, you'll find your own growth energized even further as you communicate your learning with others.

You can format your group with whatever approach helps you most. Some prefer a short lunchtime group with a 30–40 minute time of sharing. Others meet during mornings or evenings for an extended period of 60 minutes or more. Still others may prefer to use this guide for a weekend retreat or personal enrichment.

The structure has intentionally been kept simple, yet high impact. Each chapter begins with a **Getting Started** segment to help fuel your initial interaction. **Questions for Discussion** provides a helpful way to talk together about the actual content from the book. **Thoughts for Reflection** suggests various ideas to stimulate meaningful conversation based on each chapter. **Options for Application** provide specific opportunities to integrate what you've learned with your daily life. Finally, each session ends with a **Parting Shot**, leaving your group with a meaningful quote or insightful statement to summarize the group's time together.

We highly value your group's stories of life change! Please send us your stories at www.GaryChapman.org. We look forward to hearing about the difference *The Five Languages of Apology* makes in your life and the lives of those in your group.

1

Why APOLOGIZE?

GETTING STARTED: *Name some of the worst apologies you have ever heard. What made these apologies sound so ridiculous?*

Questions for Discussion

1. This chapter suggests, "Something within us cries for reconciliation." How do you feel when someone has offended you? Is your first response anger, hurt, frustration, or something else?

2. How does the idea that "the art of apology can be learned" strike you? Do you find it naturally easy or difficult to apologize when you have hurt someone?

3. A lack of apology causes us to seek justice. How have you observed this in your experiences?

Thoughts for Reflection

4. Think of a recent time you have hurt someone and then offered an apology. How did that person's attitude change?

5. Those we care about most are those most affected by our apologies. Who are the people in your life who will be most affected by your learning in the area of apology?

Options for Application

6. What are some of the worst apologies you have given—or received? Make a list of the negative aspects of these apologies; then look at the list three times over the next week, reminding yourself of the kinds of apologies you want to avoid.

7. List several reasons why someone should apologize when they have offended another person. Don't stop with two or three. Aim for ten or more. The more reasons you can offer, the more you are likely to believe in the importance of apologies in your life.

PARTING SHOT: *"Apology is a lovely perfume; it can transform the clumsiest moment into a gracious gift."*
—MARGARET LEE RUNBECK

APOLOGY LANGUAGE #1

Expressing **REGRET**

"I am sorry"

GETTING STARTED: *Robert Fulghum wrote in* All I Really Need to Know I Learned in Kindergarten: *"Say you're sorry when you hurt somebody." What other "kindergarten lessons" come to your mind that relate to apologizing? Feel free to share stories from your own childhood experiences.*

Questions for Discussion

1. What would most people say they are looking for in an apology?
2. In the story of Katie and Robert, how did Katie's body language influence the level of sincerity in her apologies to Robert?
3. How does including the details of an apology communicate an authentic apology?
4. When an apology is immediately followed by a statement of blame, how does this change the apology's impact?

Thoughts for Reflection

5. Think back to a recent time you said "I'm sorry" to another person. What were the circumstances of the situation? How did saying "I'm sorry" change the outcome?
6. In the opening story, Oliver North states, "That's not an apology . . . She didn't say 'Will you forgive me?' 'I'm sorry' is not an apology." How strongly do you agree or disagree with this statement?

Options for Application

7. Think of someone you still need to apologize to in your life. Take a few minutes to write a sincere letter of apology, providing the specific details of your offense.
8. Begin a journal or list for the next week, taking special note of instances where you apologize to others and when others apologize to you. Observe trends, impact, and changes in people as you experience the power of apology.

PARTING SHOT: *"Forgiveness does not change the past, but it does enlarge the future."*
—PAUL BOESE

CHAPTER

3

A P O L O G Y   L A N G U A G E   # 2

Accepting **RESPONSIBILITY**

"I was wrong"

GETTING STARTED: *Name a few of the most outrageous excuses you have heard people claim for refusing to admit wrong. Why do you think these people had such a difficult time admitting a wrongful act?*

Questions for Discussion

1. This chapter teaches that we often believe, "To admit that we are wrong is perceived as weakness." How does it make you feel to admit that you were wrong?

2. In the story of Joy and Rich, neither person felt they had done anything wrong. When was a time you felt you had done nothing wrong, yet someone expected an apology? How did you respond?

3. Pam's story reveals how her upbringing greatly impacted the way she viewed apologies. How has your childhood affected how you perceive the apologies of other people?

Thoughts for Reflection

4. When someone offends you and apologizes, saying, "I was wrong," how does it strike you? What emotions do you feel?

5. What do you think about this chapter's idea of using the agree/disagree approach to express emotions? How could you implement this in your life?

Options for Application

6. Take a few moments to write a fictional letter to one of your parents. What would you say to your father or mother? What issues would you need to address regarding your own wrongdoing or apologies? What consequences from their treatment of you remain unresolved? After writing the letter, choose one aspect of it to apply in your real life, whether contacting a parent or making a personal change or decision.

7. Be on the lookout in your use of rationalization. The next time you hurt or offend someone, admit the wrong immediately. Take special note of the person's reaction to share with your group.

PARTING SHOT: *"It takes a great deal of character strength to apologize quickly out of one's heart rather than out of pity. A person must possess himself and have a deep sense of security in fundamental principles and values in order to genuinely apologize."*

—STEPHEN COVEY

APOLOGY LANGUAGE #3

Making **RESTITUTION**

"What can I do to make it right?"

GETTING STARTED: *What do you think of courts offering large sums of money for reparative damages? When do you feel the awarded amounts become excessive?*

Questions for Discussion

1. This chapter suggests there is a voice within us that cries out for those who have wronged us to pay for their act. In what ways has this been true in your life? How have you sensed the need for another person to "pay for" his or her offense against you?

2. One comment included "I want him to make amends as appropriate. Things don't just go away by saying 'I'm sorry.'" How accurately does this describe your response in expecting an apology? How would you respond to this person?

3. Speaking someone's love language is central in making restitution successful. Of the five love languages (words of affirmation, acts of service, receiving gifts, quality time, and physical touch), which is most important to you? Why do you think this is the case?

Thoughts for Reflection

4. Recall a time another person offered restitution to you. How did you feel about the offer? How do you think the other person felt after offering restitution?

5. Her husband's hurtful words cut deeply, but Marti still remembers when later "he stood behind me, put his hands on my shoulders, and said . . . what he had done was wrong and he was sorry." His affirming touch brought healing. What similar story could you share based on someone responding with your love language?

Options for Application

6. Can you think of a time you publicly humiliated someone? If so, think of a way to publicly praise this person, offering a powerful opportunity to restore respect.

7. Review the statements of restitution at the end of this chapter. Choose two statements to use in specific relationship situations this week.

PARTING SHOT: *"One of the most basic principles for making and keeping peace is that there should be an honest attempt at the reconciliation of differences."*
—JIMMY CARTER

Apology Language #3: Making Restitution

5

APOLOGY LANGUAGE #4

Genuinely **REPENTING**

"I'll try not to do that again"

GETTING STARTED: *Name some of the differences you have noticed between men and women when they apologize. Why do you think these differences exist?*

Questions for Discussion

1. This chapter defines repentance as "to turn around" or "to change one's mind." In what other ways have you heard repentance defined? What do you think of the idea that repentance includes the concept of "I'll try not to do that again"?

2. Abby believes Bob is a good apologizer because he says he will try not to make the mistake again. Why does she believe this makes his apologies good?

3. In relation to Greg's story we learned, "The idea that we only need to make changes when we are doing something morally wrong is erroneous." What examples can you think of in your life?

Thoughts for Reflection

4. "The second step down the road of repentance is developing a plan for implementing change." What areas of your life need a plan for change?

5. The importance of specific plans for change is often overlooked. When making plans, it is often helpful to include friends in order to keep focused on our specific change areas. What are some ways those in your group could help encourage one another in their areas of desired change?

Options for Application

6. Create a list of at least five of the best apologies you have heard or experienced. What common themes emerge from your list? How could you use these themes in improving your apologies with others?

7. Search for an opportunity this week to include "I'll try not to do that again" with your next apology. Notice how this impacts the outcome of the situation. Be prepared to share with your group next time regarding the difference it makes.

PARTING SHOT: *"You cannot repent too soon, because you do not know how soon it may be too late."*
—THOMAS FULLER

APOLOGY LANGUAGE #5

Requesting **FORGIVENESS**

"Will you please forgive me?"

GETTING STARTED: *When was a time you thought you had apologized for a situation but later discovered the other person didn't feel that you had apologized? What further action did you take in that situation?*

Questions for Discussion

1. In Martin and Angie's story, Martin admits, "I know I did wrong . . . it's just that asking you to forgive me is so hard . . . I don't know why it's so hard!" Why do you think this act was so difficult for Martin? Why was it so important to Angie?
2. What are some of the reasons people ask for forgiveness according to this chapter? Which of these three reasons do you believe is most important? Why?
3. One of the reasons that requesting forgiveness is so challenging is due to a person's fear of rejection. How strongly does rejection influence your ability to ask forgiveness of others?

Thoughts for Reflection

4. Which of the five apology languages do you think is your primary apology language? What factors led you to decide on your particular apology language?
5. What is the difference between *requesting* that someone ask for forgiveness and *demanding* that someone ask for forgiveness?
6. How can we learn to offer forgiveness even in situations when the other person is unwilling or unable to request it?

Options for Application

7. This chapter suggests practicing the primary love language of the offending person from whom you would like to hear a request for forgiveness. If you are currently in such a situation, what are some specific actions you could take to show love toward the other person based on his or her love language?
8. Review the requests for forgiveness at the end of this chapter. Choose one to use this week in one of your important relationships.

PARTING SHOT: *"Blessed are the merciful, for they will be shown mercy."*

—JESUS (MATTHEW 5:7)

Discovering Your **PRIMARY**
Apology *Language*

GETTING STARTED: *Which of the five apology languages are most important to you? Think about your closest friend. Which apology language do you think is most important to him or her?*

Questions for Discussion

1. Jennifer argues that a husband and wife usually have different apology languages. If you are married, how does knowing this make understanding your spouse's apology language more difficult? How could it actually be helpful?
2. Jim's father had the philosophy that "Apologizing will get you nowhere. Do the best you can and don't look back." How have the attitudes of your parents affected your views toward apologies?
3. Review the questions for discovering your primary love language. Which one do you find most helpful?

Thoughts for Reflection

4. When have you responded with an apology that did not match the other person's apology language? In what ways was the power of your apology weakened?
5. What do you personally desire most in an apology? Why do you think this is the case?

Options for Application

6. Use the questions for discovering another person's primary apology language to determine the apology language of someone you know. Then share the concepts of apology languages and ask that person if he or she thinks your choice was accurate.
7. If you are in a family situation, experiment with the group project suggested in this chapter for discovering the apology languages of your family members. Take notes and try apologizing based on your discoveries.

PARTING SHOT: *"The greatest discovery of my generation is that a human being can alter his life by altering his attitudes."*
—WILLIAM JAMES

APOLOGIZING *Is*
a Choice

GETTING STARTED: *When was a time you chose to wait to apologize rather than doing it immediately? How did this affect the relationship?*

Questions for Discussion

1. What problems result from waiting to apologize to someone? How does waiting make the situation worse?
2. This chapter includes a list of reasons why people choose not to apologize. Which reason are you most likely to practice?
3. Many people form an "insensitive conscience" over time and no longer consider what they do as being wrong. How have you experienced this in your own life? In the lives of those close to you?

Thoughts for Reflection

4. How does apologizing help a person's self-esteem? In what ways does not apologizing hurt a person's self-esteem?
5. Some people consider it a difficult challenge to apologize, such as Carl as he recalled his actions before and during his mother's funeral. What factors make it seem so difficult to apologize in such a situation?
6. On the other hand, some people are overly apologetic. Why would this be the case? How could better understanding the languages of apology help?

Options for Application

7. Perhaps, like Carl, there is someone in your life you would like to apologize to, but they are no longer available, whether by death or another factor. Take an alternative approach and write an apology on paper or in a journal, personally removing this barrier from your life.
8. List some of the ways you find yourself justifying your wrong behaviors, such as saying, "He started it," or, "If she would just give me more time . . ." After identifying a few of your top responses, write what your ideal responses would be in place of these behaviors. As you catch yourself falling into old patterns, remind yourself of your ideal behaviors to help grow in forgiveness as a choice.

PARTING SHOT: *"Nobody ever did, or ever will, escape the consequences of his choices."*

—ALFRED A. MONTAPERT

Learning to FORGIVE

GETTING STARTED: *When do you find it most difficult to forgive someone? Why do you think this is the case?*

Questions for Discussion

1. How is an offense like "a bomb falling on a picnic"? In what ways can the outcome differ depending on our response?
2. Forgiveness is defined as "taking away one's sins (failures)." How would you define forgiveness in your own words?
3. In the forgiveness cycle (offense, apology, forgiveness), the choice to forgive helps complete the process. How difficult do you find it to forgive?

Thoughts for Reflection

4. Why is it dangerous to forgive too easily? How can doing so lead to destructive behavior?
5. In some situations, time is required before forgiveness is possible. What do you think is the relationship between time to forgive and trust?
6. Even when forgiveness is expressed, consequences remain. Name a situation where you forgave the offense yet remember the pain of the situation. How has the situation been difficult even with forgiveness? How is it better as a result?

Options for Application

7. Review the statements of forgiveness at the end of this chapter. Choose at least one, and use it in a situation requiring forgiveness this week.
8. Find a story that illustrates the power of forgiveness from your life or in something you have recently read. Bring the story to your group next week to share as an encouragement.

PARTING SHOT: *"Forgiveness is an act of the will, and the will can function regardless of the temperature of the heart."*
— CORRIE TEN BOOM

10

Learning to APOLOGIZE in the Family

GETTING STARTED: *What was something funny you did as a kid? How have some of your actions as a child continued to influence you today?*

Questions for Discussion

1. In Marcie's story, what made the greatest difference in changing the relationship with her parents?
2. Put yourself in the shoes of Michael in his tombstone story. What would you find most difficult? How would you have responded differently?
3. A lack of apology causes us to seek justice. How have you observed this in your experiences?

Thoughts for Reflection

4. How does apologizing to someone often result in the other person also apologizing? What examples can you think of from your own life?
5. In what ways can writing an apology statement help in dealing with an emotional issue? Can you think of a time when writing out your apology would have better helped the situation?

Options for Application

6. Make a list of your immediate and extended family members. Choose one person each week for the next month to contact in order to build a better relationship. If you discover any unresolved issues along the way, promptly apply your learning from this chapter to apologize and enhance the relationship.
7. Using the same list from the previous question, perform your best detective work to determine the primary apology language of each family member. Mentally extend this practice over the next week as you speak with friends, coworkers, and acquaintances. Notice patterns and perspectives to share with your group during your next meeting.

PARTING SHOT: *"Other things may change us, but we start and end with family."*
—ANTHONY BRANDT

Teaching Your CHILD to Apologize

GETTING STARTED: *For those with children or who inter-act with the children of others, what are some of the interesting (or foolish) things you have recently seen children do or say?*

Questions for Discussion*

1. "Perhaps I have discovered another reason why adults often find it hard to apologize—they were never taught as children." How strongly do you agree with this statement? How good do you think your child is at making apologies?
2. Review the principles listed for "what children need to know." Which of these categories do you believe is most important?
3. How can we help our children better understand "When I help people, I feel good about myself. When I hurt people, I feel badly"?

Thoughts for Reflection*

4. What are some of the rules in your house? Review this chapter's questions on determining good rules for your children (page 179). What are some rules you need to add in your family? What are some rules you could remove?
5. Why is it so difficult to consistently enforce the rules we have for our children? What can be done to help in this area with your family?
6. How do you feel about telling your children about your own apologies? What positive teaching could this provide for your son or daughter?

Options for Application

7. Ask your child what he or she says when apologizing. Then ask what other ways people apologize to one another. Use these questions to help your child see how people apologize in different ways.
8. Watch a video or read a book together that includes an apology. Ask your child questions about the story. Use it as a teachable moment for sharing about apologies.

* Readers who don't have children may choose to share their observations about other families.

PARTING SHOT: *"The best thing to spend on your children is your time."*

—LOUISE HART

Teaching Your Child to Apologize

APOLOGIZING *in*

Dating Relationships

GETTING STARTED: *Describe one of the most humorous dates you can remember. What made it so funny?*

Questions for Discussion

1. What do you think of the comment "Dating is a relationship sport"? How does the idea of dating as a sport promote a negative approach to dating?
2. Review Zack and Lindsay's story. When do you feel "enough is enough" for you in a dating relationship? What difference would applying the languages of apology make?
3. In Chad and Nina's story, how did a lack of understanding the languages of apology hurt their relationship?
4. Name some ways in which learning how to apologize well before marriage helps strengthen the future marriage relationship. If married, how did some of these ways help or hurt in the dating stages of your relationship?

Thoughts for Reflection

5. Review the stories of the three dating couples in the section "Removing the Red Flag." Which story most closely connects with a dating relationship you have experienced?
6. In what ways can a "fix-it" mentality hurt a dating relationship? In what ways can it be helpful?

Options for Application

7. If you are single, list your last two or three dating relationships and a few notes about how each one ended. Then note how the concepts you have learned about apologies could have made a difference in the situation.
8. If you are currently dating, take some time in the next week to share what you have learned in this chapter with the person you are dating. If possible, ask about working through the book together as a couple.

PARTING SHOT: *"You come to love not by finding the perfect person, but by seeing an imperfect person perfectly."*
— SAM KEEN

CHAPTER

13

APOLOGIZING *in the* Workplace

GETTING STARTED: *What has been your most embarrassing moment in your workplace?*

Questions for Discussion*

1. The opening of this chapter contrasts the differences between a positive trip to the bank and a negative encounter at the post office. What was the difference in the two situations?
2. The pizza restaurant's manager shared that his customers always get the L.A.S.T. word. How could the aspects of the L.A.S.T. word help in your workplace?
3. Have you ever had a medical professional apologize to you? What happened? How would the situation have been different if the person had not apologized?
4. When was a time you needed to apologize to a coworker? How did your apology change the situation?

Thoughts for Reflection*

5. When was a time you were unsatisfied as a customer? What kind of apology would have best improved your view of the problem?
6. Many of us spend more of our waking hours at work than anywhere else. What practical ideas could you help implement to improve the relational atmosphere of your workplace?

Options for Application

7. If possible, share the concepts of the five languages of apology with your coworkers. Do your best to learn one another's apology language and use it in future situations.
8. What would be an ideal way of handling dissatisfied customers in your workplace? Create a list. Then place it in a prominent place in your office or work environment as a regular reminder.

* Readers who don't go to a workplace may share their experiences in other social settings.

PARTING SHOT: *"Let us realize that the privilege to work is a gift, that power to work is a blessing, that love of work is success."*
—DAVID O. MCKAY

APOLOGIZING *to* Yourself

GETTING STARTED: *Why does it seem easier at times to forgive other people than to forgive ourselves? How have you seen this in your life?*

Questions for Discussion

1. In Josh's story, how did apologizing to himself complete his journey toward positive change?
2. What are some of the reasons given for wanting to apologize to yourself? Which one do you believe is most important for you?
3. "When we fail to live up to our ideal self, what happens inside of us is what happens inside others when we offend them: We become angry." What is your initial response when angry? Are you more likely to suppress or express your anger with yourself and others? What changes could best help you in this area?

Thoughts for Reflection

4. What do you think of the idea of talking with yourself about self-apology? Does it feel natural or awkward? How has your background influenced how you view this concept of self-talk?
5. Think of a recent episode when you were angry at yourself. How did you respond? In what ways do you wish you would have acted differently?

Options for Application

6. Write your own apology to yourself for any unresolved personal issues. As with Jordan's story, stand in front of the mirror and actually read it out loud to yourself.
7. After writing your apology, make note of areas you desire to change. Choose one or two areas where you seek improvement. Then talk with someone in your group about a plan of action.

PARTING SHOT: *"An apology is the superglue of life. It can repair just about anything."*
—LYNN JOHNSTON

The APOLOGY
Language Profile

The following profile is designed to help you discover your apology language. Read each of the twenty hypothetical scenarios, and check (✓) the one response you would most like to hear if that particular situation were to occur in your life. Assume that, in each scenario, you and the other person have a relationship in which it is in both of your best interests to maintain a respectful and considerate attitude. In other words, if the relationship is damaged in some way by the other person, assume that the relationship is important enough that you feel it necessary to receive the other person's apology when he/she has offended you. Also, assume that the "offender" is aware of his/her offense because you have expressed your hurt in some noticeable, direct way.

Some of the possible responses to each of the twenty scenarios are similar. Focus less on their similarity and more on choosing the response that most appeals to you, and then move on to the next item.

1. Your spouse failed to acknowledge your wedding anniversary. (If you are not married, assume you are in this scenario.) He/she should say:

   _____ ◊ "I can't believe I forgot. You and our marriage are so important to me. I am so sorry."

   _____ ○ "There is no excuse for me forgetting. What was I thinking?"

   _____ △ "What can I do to prove my love for you?"

   _____ ❑ "You can bet I won't forget next year! I'm going to circle the date on my calendar!"

   _____ ☆ "I know you are hurt, but can you ever forgive me?"

2. Your mother knew how you felt about a matter and knowingly went against your wishes. She should say:

   _____ ○ "If I had only thought about what I was doing, I would have realized it was wrong."

   _____ △ "What can I do to regain your respect?"

   _____ ❑ "I won't take your feelings for granted in the future."

   _____ ☆ "Will you please give me another chance?"

   _____ ◊ "I knew how you felt but went against your wishes anyway. I wish I had not done that."

3. You were in a crisis and needed help, but your friend ignored your need. He/she should say:

   _____ △ "Saying 'I'm sorry' doesn't feel like it is enough. What more can I say or do to mend our friendship?"

   _____ ❑ "I realize now that I could have been more help to you, and I promise that I'll do everything I can do to help you if ever you are in trouble again."

   _____ ☆ "I am sincerely sorry and ask you to forgive to me."

_____ ◊ "I should have been there for you. I'm so sorry I let you down."

_____ ○ "I let you down when you needed me the most. I made a terrible mistake."

4. Your sister made an insensitive remark about you. She should say:

_____ ❏ "While I will likely say wrong things again in the future, what I've learned from this experience will help me avoid hurting you with insensitive comments."

_____ ☆ "I blew it! Can you forgive me?"

_____ ◊ "That was so thoughtless of me. I wish I had been more considerate of your feelings."

_____ ○ "I know what I said was wrong and that I hurt your feelings."

_____ △ "Would you allow me to retract what I said? I would like a chance to restore your reputation."

5. Your spouse lashed out in anger against you when you had done no apparent wrong. He/she should say:

_____ ☆ "I am truly sorry for yelling at you. I hope that you can find it in your heart to forgive me."

_____ ◊ "I wish I had not hurt you by yelling at you. I feel so bad for how I treated you."

_____ ○ "I was angry, but I had no right to speak to you that way. You did not deserve that."

_____ △ "What can I do or say to make things right between you and me?"

_____ ❏ "I'm afraid that I'll do this again, and I don't want to. Help me think of ways to avoid blowing up like this in the future."

The Apology Language Profile

6. You were proud of your accomplishment, but your friend acted as if it was trivial. He/she should say:

_____ ◊ "You needed me to share your excitement, and I let you down. I hate that I didn't respond more appropriately."

_____ ○ "I spoiled your celebration by not being happy for you. I could make excuses, but really, I have no good excuse for ignoring your achievement."

_____ △ "Is it too late for us to celebrate your accomplishment? I really want to make this up to you."

_____ ❏ "I promise I'll notice and celebrate your accomplishments in the future. I've learned a hard lesson."

_____ ☆ "I know I failed you before, but will you please forgive me again?"

7. Your business partner failed to consult with you on an important matter of mutual interest. He/she should say:

_____ ○ "I really blew it this time. I was wrong to not include you in this decision. You have a right to be upset with me."

_____ △ "Is there anything I can do to make up for what I did?"

_____ ❏ "In the future, I plan to consult with you no matter what. I won't bypass you in making decisions again."

_____ ☆ "You have every right to hold this against me, but will you please forgive me?"

_____ ◊ "I know now that I hurt you very badly. I am truly sorry for what I did."

8. A coworker unintentionally poked fun at you and embarrassed you in front of others in your workplace. He/she should say:

_____ △ "Is there any way I can repair our relationship? Would you like for me to apologize to you in front of the staff?"

_____ ❑ "It's easy to take others' feelings for granted, but I want to be more considerate of you and others in the future. Will you help hold me accountable?"

_____ ☆ "I didn't intend to hurt you, and now all I can do is ask for your forgiveness and try not to repeat my same mistake again."

_____ ◊ "I deeply regret embarrassing you like I did. I wish I could go back in time and say something more appropriate."

_____ ○ "That was so thoughtless of me. I thought I was being funny, but obviously, hurting you like I have is not funny."

9. You were trying to tell your friend something important, and he/she acted disinterested. He/she should say:

_____ ❑ "I messed up this time, but in the future, I promise to give you my full attention when you say you have something important to tell me."

_____ ☆ "I'm sorry I wasn't listening. You don't have to forgive me, but I hope you will."

_____ ◊ "I feel really bad that I didn't listen to what you were saying. I know how it feels to have something important to say, and I regret that I didn't listen to you."

_____ ○ "Listening is such an important part of a strong relationship, but once again, I blew it. You needed me to hear you, and I basically just ignored your need."

_____ △ "Can we back up and try again? You talk, and I'll listen. You'll have my undivided attention."

The Apology Language Profile

10. Your brother learned that he had previously been wrong about a significant point of conflict between the two of you. He should say:

_____ ☆ "I apologize. Will you please forgive me?"

_____ ◊ "I am upset with myself over how I handled our disagreement. My behavior threatened our relationship, and that scares me. I regret the way I acted."

_____ ○ "I admit that I was wrong. If I had only known then what I know now, I could have saved us a lot of heartache."

_____ △ "What can I do to mend our relationship? I feel like I need to do or say something to restore your respect for me."

_____ ❏ "If we disagree over an issue in the future, I plan on gathering all the facts before I make any judgments. That may save us from unnecessary arguing."

11. Although you had expressed your annoyance with a particular habit many times before, your spouse continued exhibiting the behavior to spite you. He/she should say:

_____ ◊ "I've taken this too far. I'm very sorry for not being more considerate of your wishes. I wouldn't like it if you did that to me."

_____ ○ "OK, I admit it; I am annoying you on purpose, and that's neither funny nor fair. I need to act more mature than that."

_____ △ "Saying 'I'm sorry' won't take back the fact that I've knowingly tried to annoy you. What more can I do to win back your favor?"

_____ ❏ "I have gotten into the habit of disregarding your wishes, and I don't want to go on doing that. From now on, I'm going to make extra effort to honor your wishes."

_____ ☆ "I've tried your patience, and now I'm asking you to forgive me. Will you allow me a fresh start in honoring your requests?"

12. Your father gave you the "silent treatment" as a way of making you feel guilty about something on which the two of you disagreed. He should say:

_____ ◯ "There is no denying that I'm guilty. I should have handled the situation with more fairness and honesty."

_____ △ "I would like to make this up to you somehow, and I want to keep talking with you. May I take you out to dinner?"

_____ ❏ "In the future, I'm going to be more honest about how I feel without trying to make you feel guilty for not agreeing with me."

_____ ☆ "It's your choice, but I really do hope you will forgive me."

_____ ◊ "You are an adult, and I feel really bad about controlling your decisions. I don't want to risk damaging our relationship."

13. A business associate broke a promise and caused you to miss an important deadline. He/she should say:

_____ ❏ "It's too late to do anything about it now, but I want so badly to avoid this type of error again. Let's talk about what I can do in the future to make good on my promises."

_____ ☆ "I don't expect you to forgive me considering the trouble I've caused you, but I would greatly appreciate it if you would forgive me."

_____ ◊ "I am so sorry. I promised you I'd come through, and I not only let you down but caused you to miss your deadline. I know this jeopardizes your work and our partnership."

_____ ◯ "I've really messed up this time. You missed your deadline because of me."

_____ △ "I don't know what I can do at this point, but is there any way I can compensate you for my part in your missed deadline?"

14. Your neighbor asked you to wait on him/her outside the arena, but he/she never showed up for the concert. He/she should say:

_____ ☆ "Our friendship really is important, and I hope you won't give up on me. Will you forgive me for standing you up?"

_____ ◊ "I'm so sorry you had to stand there waiting on me. You are important to me, and I should have honored you and your time by being there when I said I would be."

_____ ◯ "You stood there waiting on me, thinking I would show up at any moment, and I let you down. If I had only managed my time differently, I would have been there. That is totally my fault."

_____ △ "Let's go to another concert, and this time, I'm paying for your ticket as a way of apologizing for standing you up last time."

_____ ❑ "In the future, I will manage my time and prioritize my schedule so that I tend to our friendship like I should."

15. A friend's child broke one of your prized possessions while visiting in your home. Your friend should say:

_____ ◊ "I know this was one of your prized possessions, and I feel terrible about what has happened."

_____ ○ "I should have been watching my child more closely. It was my fault for not paying more attention to what was going on. If I had just done a couple of things differently, this would not have happened."

_____ △ "May I pay you for this special item, or can I purchase it somewhere for you? Is there some way I can replace this?"

_____ ❏ "I promise that I will be more protective of your possessions in the future and will not allow my child to play in 'off limits' areas when we're in your home."

_____ ☆ "You have a right to be upset, but I hope that you can forgive me and remain my friend despite your disappointment."

16. A church member blamed you with sole responsibility for the failure of a committee project although he/she shared leadership duties of the committee. He/she should say:

_____ △ "There is no excuse for my behavior, and the only way I'm going to feel remotely better is to make this right between us. What do you need me to do or say?"

_____ ❏ "I'm either going to learn how to treat my team members more appropriately, or I'm not going to lead any more committees. I want to grow from this experience."

_____ ☆ "Please forgive me. I was wrong to blame you, and I pray that you will forgive me."

The Apology Language Profile

_____ ◊ "I can't believe I blamed you like I did. I really am embarrassed about my behavior, and I'm sorry."

_____ ○ "I had just as much to do with the failure of this project as you or anyone else. I should have admitted my shortcomings."

17. Despite his/her promise to keep your secret, your coworker broke your trust in him/her by telling others in the office. He/she should say:

_____ ○ "I told you I would keep your secret, and I broke my promise and damaged your trust in me. I made a terrible mistake."

_____ △ "Help me know what I should do to restore your trust in me."

_____ ❏ "It may take you some time to rebuild your trust in me, but I'll be working hard from now on to prove that I am trustworthy."

_____ ☆ "You don't have to answer immediately, but will you consider forgiving me for making this mistake?"

_____ ◊ "If only I had thought about how much damage I was doing by telling your secret. I feel so bad for not having taken my promise more seriously."

18. Your teammate spoke negatively about you to others on the team. He/she should say:

_____ △ "I want to do anything I can to correct my mistake. Shall I apologize in front of the team?"

_____ ❏ "If I am ever again upset with you, I promise to gather my thoughts and approach you directly and respectfully."

_____ ☆ "You may not be able to forgive me, at least not now, but I hope you can forgive me someday."

_____ ◊ "What I said was mean and unkind. I regret what I said, and I wish that I could take it back."

_____ ○ "I had a bad attitude and didn't once think about your positive attributes. I should have thought more about what I was saying."

19. Despite your having several positive accomplishments, your supervisor only criticized your performance. He/she should say:

_____ ❏ "You deserve recognition for your hard work. I will try to be more balanced next time."

_____ ☆ "I hope this won't damage our relationship. Will you accept my apology?"

_____ ◊ "I am so sorry that I focused on the minor flaws of your performance. I regret that I didn't encourage you more."

_____ ○ "I neglected to compliment you on the many strengths of your performance, and you may have felt that all your practice was for nothing. As your supervisor, I should be more forthcoming with praise for all the good work that you do."

_____ △ "How can I earn your forgiveness? Shall I write down the strengths of your performance?"

20. At lunch, your server dropped food on you and ruined your shirt. He/she should say:

_____ ☆ "Can you please forgive me for my carelessness?"

_____ ◊ "I am so sorry about that. I feel bad that I've ruined your shirt and inconvenienced you like this."

_____ ○ "I am normally pretty careful, but I wasn't careful enough this time. I accept full responsibility for this mess."

_____ △ "I would like to reimburse you for your dry cleaning or for the cost of a new shirt. What seems most appropriate to you?"

_____ ❑ "This has taught me a hard lesson. You can bet that I'll be even more careful in the future when serving guests."

RECORDING AND INTERPRETING YOUR SCORE

Go back and count how many times you checked each of the individual shapes. Then, transfer those totals to the appropriate columns below. For example, if you checked ❑ eight times, then write the number 8 in the blank above the ❑below.

As you may have guessed, each of the five shapes represents a certain language of apology. Thus, ◊ = Expressing Regret, ◯ = Accepting Responsibility, △ = Making Restitution, ❑ = Genuinely Repenting, and ☆ = Requesting Forgiveness. Whichever shape you circled the most times while answering the twenty profile questions is your primary language of apology.

Obviously, the highest score possible for any of the individual languages is twenty. If you scored the same amount of points for two or more languages, then you may feel equally receptive to two or more of the apology languages.

Also available in audio by Oasis Audio, **ISBN: 1-59859-149-5**,
Where Quality Speaks for Itself.
Read by Dr. Gary Chapman & Dr. Jennifer Thomas

Also available in Spanish from Oasis Audio, **ISBN: 1-59859-150-9**,
Where Quality Speaks for Itself.

ISBN: 1-4143-1289-X

The book is also available in Spanish
El libro está también disponible en Español
from Tyndale Español

THE FIVE LOVE LANGUAGES

We all want to love and be loved. But how can we learn to express that love—especially to our mate? By learning his or her "love language," says Dr. Gary Chapman. It's a message that's positive, hopeful, and easy to apply—as more than 4 million readers have already discovered.

ISBN 1-881273-15-6

Audio-CD **ISBN 1-881273-37-7**

Unabridged Audio-CD **ISBN 1-58926-906-3**

more than four million sold

THE FIVE LOVE LANGUAGES

New York Times Bestseller

THE FIVE LOVE LANGUAGES MEN'S EDITION

Men: How can you learn to speak (and understand) the love language of the woman in your life? This special edition of the bestselling *The Five Love Languages* includes new features just for men! Complete the profile and discover her and your love languages . . . then try out some of the new end-of-chapter ideas on showing heartfelt love to that special woman in your life.

ISBN 1-881273-10-5

Unabridged Audio-CD **ISBN 1-59859-066-9**

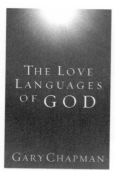

THE LOVE LANGUAGES OF GOD

How do you receive and reflect divine love? This unique book brings a new and complete understanding of how to build a closer and more loving relationship with God.

ISBN 1-881273-93-8

THE FIVE LOVE LANGUAGES FOR SINGLES

Single adults have unique needs—yet they, like everyone, also need to give love and be loved. Chapman looks at the special joys and challenges singles face, and helps them apply the five love languages to their lives—at work, in relationships, and more.

ISBN 1-881273-98-9

Unabridged audio-CD **ISBN 1-59859-113-4**

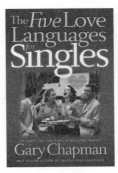

more resources on

THE FIVE LOVE LANGUAGES

speak more fluently, love more deeply

THE FIVE LOVE LANGUAGES OF CHILDREN

Kids desperately need to know they are loved. Dr. Gary Chapman teams with physician Ross Campbell, bestselling author of *How to Really Love Your Child,* to show you how to speak your child's love language . . . fluently!

ISBN 1-881273-65-2

Audio-CD **ISBN 1-881273-85-7**

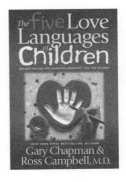

THE FIVE LOVE LANGUAGES OF TEENAGERS

It's tough to raise teens—today more than ever. Yet, says best-selling author Dr. Gary Chapman, parents, not peers, are the strongest influence on their teens. And the door to that influence is love. Using his famed five love languages principles, Dr. Chapman shares real stories and expert wisdom to encourage you as you rear—and love—your teen.

ISBN 1-881273-39-3

Audio-CD **ISBN 1-881273-78-4**

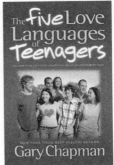

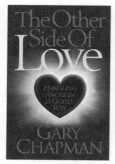

THE OTHER SIDE OF LOVE

Many of us need help with anger. But can anger be used for good?
Yes, says Dr. Gary Chapman, who shows us how we can move
anger "from one side to another"—toward love.

ISBN 0-8024-6777-6

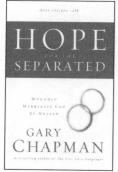

HOPE FOR THE SEPARATED

A realistic and compassionate look at the problems and
perspectives of separated couples, challenging them to explore
reconciliation.
More than 200,000 sold.

ISBN 0-8024-3639-0

LOVING SOLUTIONS

Are you living in a seriously flawed marriage? Gary Chapman
offers hope. Discover practical and permanent solutions and take
positive steps to change your marriage. Recipient of the Gold
Medallion Book Award.

ISBN 1-881273-91-1

FIVE SIGNS OF A LOVING FAMILY

In modern Western culture, it is widely acknowledged that the family is in serious trouble. Despite the odds, your desire is to have family relationships that are fully loving and functional. If you want to establish healthy patterns in your own family, you'll need to learn how to recognize and apply the qualities healthy families share.

ISBN 1-881273-92-X

more resources from

GARY CHAPMAN

New York Times Bestselling Author

WORLD'S EASIEST GUIDE TO FAMILY RELATIONSHIPS

An easy-to-use and comprehensive guide to creating and maintaining healthy relationships with your spouse and children. Includes interactive material for couples, frequently asked questions, and test-your-knowledge sections.

ISBN 1-881273-40-7

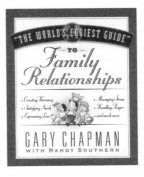

PARENTING YOUR ADULT CHILD

Few resources are available to help parents communicate with their child who is no longer a child. Here's a tool that will help you deal with such issues as: Helping Your Child Find Success, When Adult Children Return with Their Children, and more.

ISBN 1-881273-12-1

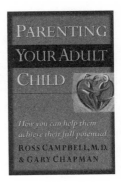

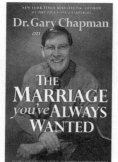

DR. GARY CHAPMAN ON
THE MARRIAGE YOU'VE ALWAYS WANTED

How does a couple "become one"—whatever their stage of marriage? And what are some of the issues that block that oneness? With the practical encouragement that has made him a bestselling relationship expert, Gary Chapman looks at such challenges as open communication, sexual fulfillment, money management, dealing with extended family, and much more.

ISBN 0-8024-8786-6

Unabridged audio-CD **ISBN 1-59859-008-1**

more resources from

GARY CHAPMAN

New York Times Bestselling Author

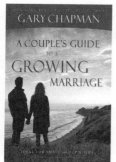

A COUPLE'S GUIDE TO
A GROWING MARRIAGE

A perfect study complement to *The Marriage You've Always Wanted,* this interactive, practical resource is designed to help couples grow closer to each other—and closer to God. Couples will discuss and reflect on such areas as money, anger, forgiveness, and spirituality, all in an easy-to-use workbook format.

ISBN 0-8024-7299-0

LOVE TALKS FOR FAMILIES

One of the signs of a healthy family is open and meaningful communication. But how do you find something the whole family can talk about together? *Love Talks* gives you 101 questions to facilitate this process in a convenient, spiral-bound booklet.

ISBN 1-881273-49-0

Also available:

Love Talks for Couples

ISBN 1-881273-48-2

More Love Talks for Couples

ISBN 1-881273-50-4

Visit www.GaryChapman.org to receive a daily e-mail from
Dr. Chapman on practical ideas for stimulating marital growth. More
information and resources are also available at fivelovelanguages.com